6/3/14

This book contains some of my clients' stories. The names have been changed, and the circumstances of each incident have been altered so individuals are not recognizable.

D1502169

FAMILY TALK

FAMILY TALK

CHRISTY MONSON

Published by Familius LLC,

Familius books are available at special discounts for bulk
purchases for sales promotions, family or corporate use. Special
editions, including personalized covers, excerpts of existing books,
or books with corporate logos, can be created in large quantities for
special needs. For more information, contact Premium Sales at
559-876-2170 or email specialmarkets@familius.com

Library of Congress Catalog-in-Publication Data
2014936356

pISBN 978-1-938301-79-7
eISBN 978-1-938301-64-3

Printed in the United States of America
Edited by Amanda Wind
Cover design by David Miles
Book design by Kurt Wahlner

10 9 8 7 6 5 4 3 2 1

First Edition

Dedication

I am grateful to my husband, Robert Monson, and our children, Kirsten Slaugh, Robin Condie, Laura Vaden, Rebekah Murcray, Christian Monson, and Rachel DeVore. They are dedicated to their families and are productive members of society. For that I am thankful. Without them this book would not be possible.

I also appreciate my critique group members, who have read and reread every page of this book, giving sound advice and helpful ideas to make this the best it can be: Margot Hovley, Chris Miller, Cory Webb, Jeanette Wright, Ken Lee, Marion Jensen, and Colin Murcray.

Thanks to the editor, Amanda Wind, for her terrific organizational skills. She has had an impact for good on this manuscript.

Preface

This book is an exposition on synergy in the family—a "how to" for creating family talk through the medium of family councils to bring about that synergy. If families work together to infuse themselves with honest, positive energy, they can create harmony, allowing and encouraging each member to become more than they could be on their own.

Dating and courtship begin for many of us when we are young. Friendship blossoms into love and marriage. Children bless our alliance with more affection as our family grows.

Families come in all different varieties. There are traditional families with a mother and father—both parents may be income-producing in some families, while others have one source of revenue. Some households have only a single parent, and working together is a must to keep life running smoothly. Others are faced with the difficulty of blending a family. Trying to mold different lifestyles into a single functioning unit of love can seem like a daunting task.

No matter what the parameters, synergistic families are based on devotion and trust—in other words, love. Encouraging communication through listening, understanding, playing together, boundary-setting, and creating rules brings deeper bonding and greater affection.

Family councils can improve relationships, increase our understanding of each other, and assist us in fostering a respectful, pleasant environment for everyone in the home—whatever our age or situation may be. In this book, we'll explore some of the important messages and skills family council meetings teach children.

In 1981, my husband and I had six children at home. They ranged in age from three to sixteen. Loving and nurturing this group of youngsters that I adored seemed like an overwhelming task some days. Somehow we smoothed our lives out with weekly family council meetings. We looked at our problems, talked about them, brainstormed solutions, and came up with actions to keep our lives somewhat intact.

When our children were older, I went back to school to become a marriage and family therapist. I have used the same positive relationship model we fostered with our children in my work with clients over the years.

Contents

Introduction

My preschooler was through with her naps, but my grandmother, Nana, usually spent an hour sleeping every afternoon. I peeked into the bedroom to see if she was still resting. Nana's eyes were open with her jaw dropped. She wasn't breathing. I touched her cheek. It was cool. Her face had a look of peace about it that I hadn't seen before—almost an angelic aura. I leaned against the wall.

Nana, age 99 years and 7 months, had just died in our home. Disbelief, shock, grief, and an overwhelming sense of "What am I going to do now?" engulfed me. She was my second mother from the time I was six years old, after my father died.

I sat down in the living room and put my head in my hands. I had to handle this. Deep breaths. Rest a minute and think. What did I need to do? How was I going to tell everyone?

My mind wandered to the many hours Nana spent reading to me when I was a child. Neither of us could get through *Lassie Come Home* without tears. I worked in the garden with her, weeding the flowerbeds. We canned fruit together, using mountains of sugar, spilling a little here and a little there until the floor was so sticky our feet squeaked as we walked. She was infinitely patient with me, teaching me to sew and cook. I knew she loved being with me.

In the background I heard the postman slip the mail through the slot. My world seemed to have stopped, but everything around me continued.

After I married, our family had spent a lot of time vacationing at Nana's home over the years, so the children also had many memories with her. They made rhubarb pies together. They played checkers by the hour, and she was always willing to read them a story—until she fell asleep. The listener would gently shake her shoulder, and she would rouse and say, "Now where was I?" and begin again.

I shifted my weight on the couch and stared out the window into the sunshine. I wondered about the afterlife. Where was Nana? What was she doing right now?

She had come to live with us three years ago, and we took care of her now—fixing her meals, washing her clothes, and bathing her—instead of her caring for us. Kirsten, age 16, enjoyed painting Nana's nails and curling her hair, and Nana loved the attention. She and Kirsten shared a room. When Nana first arrived, her mind was sharp, but as she approached the century mark, her thinking became less clear. She believed Kirsten was "the lady from New York" who didn't keep the room very tidy.

Robin, age 13, cleaned Nana's dentures every day. Robin enjoyed dropping the little blue capsule into the glass of water and watching it foam into fizzy bubbles. She helped Nana dress and settled her in her wheelchair.

Laura, age 12, loved creating fun and games for her younger siblings, and Nana joined right in. The kids would seat Nana in the recliner in the living room and then take turns pushing each other around the house in her wheelchair.

Rebekah, age 8, and Rachel, age 3, played dolls with Nana. Nana and the girls made up names for themselves, like Mrs. Fall and Mrs. Winter. Sometimes the dolls caught the measles or whooping cough. Mrs. Fall and Mrs. Winter rocked them and cared for them until they were well. Other times everyone dressed for a party in their best ball gowns and traveled to New York for a birthday celebration

When Chris was a toddler, he loved his bottle. When we decided it was time for him to give it up, Nana made a pig out of the modeling clay that the kids were playing with one day and told him, "The piggy ate your bottle." He didn't ever wonder about his bottle or ask for it again. He accepted that it was gone, and he knew what had happened to it.

During the days before her death, Nana read to the younger children, and sometimes they read to her. They wheeled her chair out by the pool where she loved to watch the kids dive and do tricks.

And now I had to explain that she was gone. What would they think? How would they feel? Every time we were in the car and passed a graveyard, the kids held their breath and lifted their feet off the floor so no dead spirits would get into them. They were sure to remember this.

Rachel walked into the living room and climbed onto my lap. "Time for Nana to get up from her nap and read me a story."

My heart sank. What should I say? I couldn't tell her just yet. I rocked her, stalling for time. "Nana's still sleeping."

The grade-school kids banged the back door open and plunked their lunch boxes on the kitchen counter.

"Let's ask Nana for her hearing aids so we can listen from far away," said Chris.

"If you get them, I get the wheelchair," said Rebekah.

"I want a ride, too," said Rachel.

The three older girls came in from school just as my husband, Bob, walked in the door.

I looked up at him, pulled him aside, and whispered, "Nana's dead."

Kirsten heard me. She and Bob went to check.

They came back into the living room and sat on the couch. Bob put his arm around me. The rest of the children gathered on the floor. I could feel the strength of the family fill me with courage I hadn't had a few minutes ago. I looked at Bob. "I want to tell them."

I swallowed the lump in my throat and looked around at the children. "Nana's gone."

Laura looked up questioningly.

"To Heaven," said Kirsten.

Tears slipped from Rebekah's eyes. She came for a hug. "I'm so sad."

I began to weep. "I'm sad, too."

"I will miss her, but I'm not sad," said Kirsten. "I know she's happier now. Her old body was so tired."

"It'll be lonesome without her," said Laura. "We had so much fun together."

"Can we go see her?" asked Chris. "I never saw a dead body."

"I don't want to see her dead," said Laura. "I want to remember her alive."

"I want to say good-bye," said Robin.

I hugged Rachel, the littlest one, while she cried.

"Everyone can choose whether to see her or not," I said.

Those who wanted to went to the bedroom to say their good-byes.

Everyone returned, and we knelt for a family prayer, expressing our gratitude for this wonderful life that had touched us in so many ways. A spirit of peace and comfort filled the room, as if Nana were still very close.

We all talked about Heaven and how beautiful it must be. The children shared their feelings. We knew Nana would be happy there.

As I watched the family interact, it was a moment in time where Heaven felt closer than ever. It was almost tangible. As the day wore on, we dealt with the coroner, funeral arrangements, babysitters, travel plans, long distance preparations, and the complications of normal daily plans thrown into the mix. But by the time I went to bed that night, everything was arranged, and, thanks to everyone's cooperation, I felt peaceful.

There was an energy in our family that day that made me better than I thought I could be—a force that inspired me to overcome my fear and feelings of being overwhelmed.

It's now been quite a few years since Nana died, but whenever we refer to it, all of our children have a significant recollection of that day and time. It's indelibly fixed in our memories as a spiritual, soul-expanding experience that has made us all better.

I have often thought of the synergy we created as a group that day. There have been many occasions as we have worked together in family councils—sometimes talking in scheduled meetings or discussing things in spontaneous gatherings like this one—when I have felt that same unity and alliance. It's an ongoing feeling of togetherness duplicated through the years whenever our family comes together, and we are all better people because of that togetherness.

Our lives haven't been perfect. We've had our problems, but incidents like this one have infused our lives with positive energy, and we are all stronger for having worked together. Now we are a larger extended family, and we gather for vacations, reunions, religious ceremonies, marriages, and deaths. But the feeling of synergy is always there, making us greater than we could be on our own.

CHAPTER 1

A Family Council: What Is It?

⤷ DEFINITION ↶

A family council is a meeting where the entire family comes together as a cooperative unit to give each other positive feedback, discuss problems, set up the week's activities, study together, or just play games. For our family, it was a means of teaching us to talk and work together as a cohesive unit. We loved, laughed, and played together, and it smoothed out the rough edges for our family of eight and saved me from going crazy on many a day.

As a marriage and family therapist, I worked with many families. The incidents throughout the book have come from my practice, my own family, and incidents friends have related.

Since the family is the basic unit of society, it's important to start there to establish an atmosphere of friendship and equal opportunity—a place where every member can be heard and valued. What an advantage for a child to begin life with so much opportunity!

As you read this book, do the following:

* Look for ways that you can bring your family closer together.
* Find ways to create a positive environment in your family.
* Practice discussing and solving problems.

The constructive energy generated by your family councils may not revolutionize the world, but your children just may.

❧ Meeting Structure ❧
Logistics: Time, Place, and Date

Sit down together as a family group to organize your meetings. Find a place where everyone can be comfortable and pay attention.

Establish a definite hour for your assembly. Choose a time when everyone can be present and everyone is rested. Stay away from late-night meetings when members may be tired.

Most families I have worked with meet once a week, but you may decide to get together more or less often. If your children are very young, you could spread some of the activity over two or more informal sessions.

Keeping the Meeting Short

Depending on the age of your children and their ability to focus, you may need to adjust the length of your gathering. Some families with older and younger children meet once for problem-solving and weekly scheduling, and then they hold a second meeting for study and activities.

Rotating the Chairperson

We found it lots of fun to let each member have a turn conducting. Ask the group to decide who will begin and what the order of the rotation will be. Even small children can lead the meeting—sometimes with the help of a parent or an older sibling.

The Smiths were a blended family with a wide mix of ages. When Dad suggested that everyone have a turn to conduct the meeting, the older teens scoffed at the idea.

"Four-year-old Sally can't lead a discussion," said Sam, the seventeen-year-old.

"Would you like to help her?" asked Mom.

Sam caught his breath, taken aback by the inquiry. He thought for a minute and said, "Yes."

Sally was shy at first about being in charge, but Sam prompted her in a gentle, kind way. As the months went by, she got so she could conduct the meeting alone except for a little help reading the agenda.

KEEPING THE MINUTES

This is one of the best parts of family councils. Keep a notebook with the minutes, and have everyone take a turn as scribe. It's so much fun to look back in a few years and read the record. You can see how your family has grown and remember precious moments you had together. It's as good as a photo album and sometimes even better because little funny happenings and sayings recorded there remind you of forgotten years.

FAMILY PERSONALITY

Every family has its own personality. Some families are casual and easygoing in handling problems. Some are more rule-bound in their approach to parenting. Some families can be very goal-oriented, while others live life as it comes.

Communication patterns are different in families. There are "hot" families who love to debate and argue with each other. I've seen families that are playful and teasing, and others that are formal and proper. Then there are families that discuss everything, and others don't talk a lot.

Take a little time to think about what the personality of your family is like. Don't be limited by the few styles I've mentioned. Use the words that best describe your family and the way it works.

Each one of the factors you describe will influence the way your family handles situations that arise. Then you can decide what your long-term goals are in raising your children. What kind of synergy do you want to create? What do you stand for? How do you want to organize yourselves?

While you are defining your family personality, decide how you will discuss your ideas with your children. Depending on their ages, let them know the strengths and weaknesses of your family. It will help the kids identify who they want to become. According to a *New York Times* article, "Stories That Bind Us," March 15, 2013, children are able to face challenges better if they know about their family. This information increases resilience in children because they have a sense of being part of a larger group.

SETTING FAMILY GOALS

Families are all goal-directed, whether or not they realize it. What you think and plan, you become. Take some time to talk as a family. It's important to define your values and the direction you want to go. If you don't set a course, you waft along wherever life takes you.

We as adults can look back and see our lack of direction and change our actions, but children don't have any history as a point of reference. If they are to be productive adults, we must teach them.

Families with older children will enjoy including everyone in setting goals. Your kids will be much more invested in your decisions if they are involved in the entire process. In my work with families, I found that when children are included, the family comes up with significant goals and great follow-through.

Making a plan is like a having road map to take the family where you want it to go.

CREATE A MISSION STATEMENT

Your family could go a step further, if you wish, and write your own mission statements. What is your purpose as a family? What is your reason for existing? Take a little time and decide your core intentions.

Your mission statement will set the overarching course of action for your goals. Long-term objectives such as service or community interaction can help your family become centered on others and foster a sense of self-esteem in your kids.

As you identify the core standards of your family, let them reflect your personal values and the ideals of your ancestors. Kids need to know how they connect to the extended family. It's even fun to reframe the more exotic ethics of your past. I know a family that had a pirate for an ancestor. They included the values of assertiveness (instead of swash-buckling) and adventurous (instead of thievery). Be creative.

COLLECTIVE AND INDIVIDUAL GOALS

In this whole process, family council is a great place not only for the family to set goals but also for the individual to make and revisit his or her own goals as the weeks and months go by. It's important to exemplify this for your children.

Once a month at the end of our family meetings, we discussed our aspirations and evaluated our progress. Family council was a time when everyone could reflect on objectives and reset goals—either privately or with the group.

SET LONG-TERM GOALS

It's fun to dream and plan big. Make long-term goals that are based on the values that are important to you. As a family, start with a five-year plan, and set yearly goals to support your objectives. After you have established your family goals, each person may decide to set personal long-term goals. It's great for adults to model this for children. Parents empower children by helping them realize they can set a direction for themselves and achieve their wishes.

Be Sure Your Short-Term Goals Support Your Long-Term Goals

Help everyone set weekly short-term goals that are consistent with their yearly long-term goals. If your child wants to learn to play the flute and join the concert band for a long-term goal, he or she has to have music lessons and practice every day for the short term. If a first grader wants to be a good reader, he or she has to read out loud to someone every day.

Set Your Goals According to Family Interests

Your goals will vary from time to time depending on family passions and talents. For several years our family memorized scriptures or wise sayings as part of our family council. We read together each day. Individual kids also had service goals, music goals, scholastic goals, etc.

As a child becomes a teenager, you won't have to check on homework or reading assignments anymore if you have been consistent in setting goals when they were young. He or she will get the work done and remember band or ball practices without being reminded.

It's a freeing feeling when kids grow to this point. While you may be sad to see your child become independent, you know you have done your work as a parent, and your child is getting ready to find their own way in the world. Children can now set their own goals.

Be Flexible in Planning

If the wind blows a different direction, adjust your sails to meet your needs. There are many things that can take us off task, like a broken leg, a job transfer, or any number of other things. Sometimes life just happens, and we need to recalculate our goals to our new circumstances.

When two of our girls were in high school, they shared their swimming goals with their high school team. My husband received a job transfer to another city where there was no high school swimming. The girls, sadly, reset their goals in another direction. It was a gloomy time for all of us because we loved those swim meets. They had become a big part of our lives.

Teens are resilient, however, and our girls focused on their music goals and became very active in their church activities, fitting in to their new lives in a timely manner. They still found time for swimming workouts, but they were not part of a team.

As your children set and achieve goals and grow to adulthood, they will have the skills as teachers to direct a classroom, or as businessmen to become chairman of the board. Whatever they decide to do with their adult lives, they will be able to set goals and achieve their dreams.

Teach your child that goals change your world

COMPLIMENTS ALL AROUND

At the beginning of each of your gatherings, ask your children to give compliments to each member of the family. This promotes a mind-set of being a cohesive unit.

Be creative in the way you organize this part of the meeting. Here are some suggestions:

* Everyone can give positive feedback to each member of the family.
* Choose a special person of the week to highlight.
* Have each person draw a name out of a jar and have them give compliments to that person only.

Optimism like this starts the meeting on a constructive note, and it's fun to see what everyone comes up with. In our family, this helped us become aware of the good things others did for us.

At first this might be awkward for the children, and they might say things like, "Erica has pretty hair," or "I like Justin's new shoes."

Encourage them during the week to watch for things they can talk about—even little things like Jane passing the butter at the dinner table. This kind of activity emphasizes the positive and encourages cooperation.

Discuss the fact that compliments don't necessarily need to be tied to an action. Explain that sometimes we give people feedback just because we love them, such as "I like having Jessica for my little sister," or "I'm glad he's my big brother."

As the children get used to doing this, they will be more sincere in what they say. It isn't just an assignment to hurry and "get over with." They have to stop and take a little time to reflect on the good traits of everyone in the family.

RESOLUTION AGENDA

Use a notebook, a bulletin board, or just a piece of paper tacked to the fridge for family members to list their names if they want to talk about a problem that needs a solution. There will be many incidents in the following pages that talk about the agenda.

During the week, if Robin tattled to me that Laura had taken a shirt from her closet or used her hair brush, I told her to put her name on the agenda, and we would discuss it at family council. The first few weeks we held family council, the lists were very long, but soon the children learned to solve many of their problems themselves.

Here's an example of a family council agenda:

Name	Problem
Mom	Toys left in the middle of the living room
Dad	Tools not returned to the garage
Jane	No chips left for school lunches
Barry	Need a ride home from baseball practice on Thursday
Evan	I want the dog to sleep on my bed this winter
Mom	Dog needs a bath

At the family council, the chairperson calls on each individual listed on the agenda and asks whether they want to discuss their difficulty or whether they have solved it. Sometimes the immediate dilemma may have been taken care of. (Evan may have returned the hammer from the tree house he was building to the garage.) But the family may still want to talk about the problem and decide if there is a general rule needed concerning this as an ongoing predicament.

SOLVING PROBLEMS

Be sure this section of your meeting doesn't turn into a blame game or a "he said/she said" bash. If the conversation turns this direction, gently bring it back by asking, "What can we do to solve this problem? What can we do to prevent this from happening again?"

Encourage your family to brainstorm possible solutions. Include everyone's ideas, even if they seem unusable. Keep a record of these in your minutes book. Talk about each entry, and decide which solution will be the most doable.

Vote on your decision. Many of the countries in the world are democracies, and it would seem that a democracy would be a good way to run a family. However, in my experience, it's best for the family to come to a consensus on an issue.

What if everyone can't agree? Table the item until the next family council to give a longer cooling-off period. Emotions are probably still too high concerning the subject to make an objective decision.

What if the children come up with an idea that the parents know won't work? Perhaps it would it be okay to let them carry the vote and try their way for a week. If their solution doesn't take care of the problem, the item will need to be discussed the next week, but the next time the children will have more knowledge to help them come to a decision.

When the Resolution Agenda
Becomes the Catalyst for a Fight

When we first organized our family councils and put the agenda up, it took a while for the kids to adjust to the concept. Things got worse before they got better. The agenda even became the vehicle for a fight. Here's what happened:

I explained to the children that I would put up an agenda. If they had any problems they wanted to talk about, they could put their names on the agenda, and they'd be able to discuss it at family council. Everyone thought this was a great idea.

Name	Problem
Mom	Messy kitchen from after-school snacks
Dad	Missing bicycle repair tools
Robin	After-school play practices
Laura	Swim meet Saturday
Chris	Rachel took my rad racer
Rachel	Chris swiped my new book
Chris	Rachel ripped off my soccer trophy
Rachel	Chris took my new hair clips
Chris	Rachel swiped my tennis racket
Rachel	Chris stole my new princess bed spread
Chris	Rachel tore the car posters off my wall

As you can tell, there was a fight going on—a fairly big one, since the kids were demolishing each other's bedrooms. Both of them were so mad that the agenda was ripped in half at this point. By this time I'd intervened—asking each to take a time-out until they were calm enough to talk through the problem. Just then, Chris's friends came by and invited him to come play soccer with them at the school. Chris wanted to go, but he knew he couldn't until he and Rachel had worked through their problem. (This was great motivation for him to get things resolved quickly.)

As the three of us sat down to talk, Chris apologized and said next time he could let Rachel play with some of his race cars if she asked first. Rachel apologized also and said next time she would be sure to ask before she took his cars. (When resolving a problem, I always asked each child to figure out what they can do next time to avoid their problem.)

Then, before Chris could go play soccer, both children needed to put everything back the way it was before the fight started. Finally, Rachel taped the agenda back together.

When it was time for family council that week, they both said they had taken care of their difficulties. Sometimes the problem can be solved in the moment, but at times it may need to wait to be discussed at the council meeting. Use your best judgment on this issue. Decide what you want to teach your children and which forum would be best.

> ## "A friend is someone who knows all about you and loves you just the same."
>
> —*ELBERT HUBBARD*

WEEKLY RESPONSIBILITIES

We had job charts that we rotated for each week of the month. If someone had a problem with the jobs allocated, they could bring it up at the meeting. Once in a while we decided to redo the assignments. If the children tired of the way things were organized, they had to come up with new ideas. We used a grid assignment chart for a while. Then we changed to a larger wheel with the jobs written on them, hooked to a smaller inside wheel with everyone's names on it. We rotated it every week so the jobs were different during the month. You can also use a bowl with a list of jobs in it, and the kids can pull out three for the week. There are many ways to do this, and it's great to see the kids' creativity at work.

As the children grew older, school and sports dictated reorganization so that everyone could get their work done. When Chris joined the swim team, he couldn't help get dinner ready and set the table because he had practice until six o'clock. We rearranged the assignments so he could load the dishwasher after dinner.

TAILORING YOUR FAMILY COUNCILS

All families are a little different. They create their own way of doing things, and that's great. It's been enlightening for me to work with families over the years and see the way they work together.

No family is perfect. We all have our problems. But life runs more smoothly if we proactively choose the direction we want to go and make sure we stay on the path by reflecting often on our goals. This is the way one family I worked with in therapy solved a difficult situation.

One afternoon, the three Taylor brothers, ages 8, 10, and 12, decided to play war. The boys made a pile of "mud bombs" in the backyard. They showed their dad how much fun they were having and explained the different tactics of their battle. They wished they had a tree fort so they could drop air bombs.

Later, when the parents went out to dinner, the boys brought "war" inside the house because they wanted to release their air bombs on the second story deck of the house. The boys threw the bombs in the house along the way to the deck. The place was quite a mess by the time Mom and Dad got home.

The boys met their parents at the door to say they were sorry. They had tried to clean up by themselves, but they hadn't done a very good job.

Mom was angry at first. She put her name on the agenda and called an emergency family meeting in one hour (she needed time to cool down). Mom couldn't stand to have her house destroyed like that. She and Dad took a walk.

At first she wanted to force the kids to vote to clean the whole thing up all by themselves. It would be a good logical consequence, she told herself. When kids make a mess, they have to clean it up.

Mother's anger could have turned a simple consequence into a punishment. I am using the term 'punishment' here as a negative form of discipline as opposed to lovingly teaching a child about the results of their actions. Our demeanor defines the degree of negative energy we put into our children's actions.

Dad thought this was an opportunity to have the family work together. The boys had already banded together to clean up. After all, he reminded her, "When I spilled milk all over the floor last week, you and I worked together to clean it up."

They decided that their goal in holding family council was to . . .

Help the family pull together as a cohesive unit.

The situation could have turned into an angry yelling match, but because the parents took a little while to decide what their long-term goals were, the situation could be resolved in a spirit of family fellowship.

While they walked, Mom relaxed. Cleaning up together was a good idea. This thought crossed her mind:

You don't have to make a child feel bad in order to do something good.

As everyone settled in for the meeting, Mom took a deep breath and shared her problem with the family. The boys said the game got away from them. They didn't realize what they were doing until they had created the mess. They didn't like dirt all over the house either.

"What are we going to do?" Mom asked.

The boys said they would clean up the mud.

Dad suggested the family work together.

The boys said that would be very nice. They would like some help.

Dad wondered what the family could do to prevent it happening again.

They brainstormed:

* Get a babysitter next time, even though the boys were old enough to tend themselves.
* Decide a secret signal to use if anyone in the family sees a problem in the making.
* Hire a housekeeper to clean up the mess. (The person creating the mess has to pay.)
* Make a new rule that the boys would not be allowed outside if the parents were gone.
* Keep outside games outside.

After some discussion, they voted to keep their outside games outside, and they all worked together to clean up. They didn't want to have to scrub dirt off the floor like that again. Dad suggested he help the boys build the tree fort to play in so they didn't have to use the deck for their air bombs. The boys decided (on their own) they would do extra chores during the week since Mom and Dad had helped them. Mom was very surprised at that offer and asked them specifically what they would like to do. They volunteered to each do a batch of laundry.

Dad said he liked the idea of a secret signal they could use at any time—even in public—if anyone saw problems coming. The kids thought it would be fun to have a hush-hush family word. After some deliberation, they decided that if any one of them said the word, everyone needed to take a quick assessment of their behavior to see if it would bring trouble. They decided to say the word "bombs" in honor of the air bomb incident.

This situation could have turned into a yelling match with punishment. But the parents . . .

* Took a time out
* Shared the problem at family council
* Listened to the boys' suggestions
* Solved the problem together

An apparent disaster was turned to an exercise in family togetherness under the direction of wise parents.

This family believed in doing things together more than some I worked with. Since the parents helped the boys clean up, the children volunteered to help with extra chores in return. The children mirrored the disposition of the parents, showing that thoughtful goal-setting by the parents paid off in setting a positive tone in the family.

Here is another example of a family I worked with in therapy. They handled a similar incident in a little different way.

The Jones family went to visit their grandparents for a long weekend. Grandma Jones had several fruit trees in the back yard. Sally, age 8, and Leslie, age 6, loved to play with their dolls in the orchard. The peaches were just ripe. They each picked one for a tea party and, after the party, decided to outline a house with ripe peaches the way children sometimes outline one with sticks or rocks. The peaches were handy so they used them. The girls constructed a living room, family room, kitchen, and bedrooms. Then they ran to get their parents to see the completed house.

Father was upset because they had picked a lot of the ripe fruit that Grandma was going to can the next day. The girls were so engrossed in their play and didn't realize what they were doing. Grandma said it was fine; she didn't mind. But Mother said her daughters needed to learn to think about what they were doing. The fruit on the ground was bruised, and some of it had been stepped on.

The family sat down for an informal council meeting to discuss the matter. When Mother asked the children how they could solve the problem, the girls replied like most kids do: "I don't know."

The family began to brainstorm ideas of how to solve the problem:

* Grandma suggested that they just all forget it. Kids would be kids.
* Grandpa said he would clean up the mess so the rats wouldn't get into it.
* Sally said they should pick up all the fruit, not Grandpa.
* Leslie said she couldn't do that. She needed help.
* Mother suggested the girls work together to pick up the fruit.
* Father said the girls should buy some more fruit for Grandma to can.
* Leslie said they didn't have any money.
* Grandfather said they could help Grandma can the remaining fruit to pay for it.
* Sally really liked that idea.

The family voted. This time they included Grandma and Grandpa since it was their home and their fruit. Everyone voted for the girls to clean up the fruit by themselves, except Leslie, who said she couldn't do it. Father encouraged her by telling her she was growing up like her big sister. When Leslie saw how everyone else voted, she decided maybe she was old enough to do the work.

The sun was hot later that day, and flies buzzed over the rotting fruit. Leslie's hands got slimy, and she didn't like it. Mother brought her a drink of water and told her she was doing a great job.

Grandma said it was "unconscionable" to make a child work so hard in the scorching sun, but she would follow the family's plan. Father suggested Grandpa take Grandma to town to get some canning supplies.

When the girls finished, Father helped them dispose of the garbage and took them to a fruit stand to replace the peaches they had picked. When they got home, the girls helped Grandma can them. The three of them had a wonderful time in the kitchen together. The girls got to taste the delicious peaches while Grandma told stories about drying fruit when she was a girl. Leslie poured the sugar into the kettle of syrup, and Sally took the pits out of the fruit while Grandmother took the skins off the peaches and put the fruit in the jars.

At the end of the canning session, the floor was so sticky it needed to be scrubbed. Grandpa said he would scrub it since he suggested the girls help with the canning.

If Grandma had had her way, she would have cleaned the mess up by herself, allowing the girls to play and turning this situation into a rescue operation. But the adults . . .

* All supported each other
* Had a goal to help the girls learn about work
* Allowed the girls to become responsible for their actions
* Modeled working together with each sharing responsibility

Let's look at the similarities in the way the Taylor and the Jones families handled their incidents. Both of them . . .

* Were kind and considerate of their children
* Were constructive in their actions
* Fostered a spirit of cooperation within the family
* Taught their children valuable work skills

* Taught the children to be responsible for their actions
* Let the children know their ideas were valued

What were the differences?

* The Taylor family worked with their children to clean up the house and build the fort.
* The Taylor parents took a time-out to get control of their feelings.
* The Jones family allowed the children to take care of the orchard themselves.
* The Jones family worked together canning the fruit.
* The Taylor children cooperated with each other from the beginning, so no further action in this area was necessary.
* The Jones family averted the potential problem of Leslie's helplessness by encouraging the girls to work together.

Goals hold us accountable.

FAMILIES WITH YOUNG CHILDREN

Family councils are effective with small children when the meetings are short and fun. After compliments and problem solving, take some time to read stories together, play favorite games, and dance (our kids loved to dress up and dance to Grieg's "In the Hall of the Mountain King" and Dvorak's *Slavonic Dances*). Sometimes just spending the evening at a local park and letting the children play is a great wrap-up to the day.

As we played games together or read with each other, our love became stronger. After all, the goal of family councils is to help everyone enjoy each other and develop greater love.

FAMILIES WITH TEENS

Listen, listen, listen. Teens will give you the feedback you need to hold a successful meeting. Let them draft chore schedules. Ask their advice, and put them in charge of activities. Organizing an event will teach your youth more than you could by coordinating it yourself. Study things they are interested in as a family. Praise their efforts, not their accomplishments.

Always include food in your time together. You'll never go wrong with pizza or doughnuts—but you already know that.

As the children get older, your meetings will become more sophisticated. Scheduling has to be coordinated. When we had teens, we didn't have enough cars for everyone, and getting everybody where they needed to go became a little tricky sometimes. Family council was a great place to plan our complicated carpooling schedule. Agendas and family goals will change over the years as the family matures.

Some families have older children and younger ones. In this situation, there is a great opportunity for the older children to mentor the younger ones. I've seen older teens play games with younger children or play the piano for them to dance. Then, after the little ones are in bed, the older children and parents can discuss the information pertinent to them. Other families have separate meetings for older children and younger ones. Every family must find the way that works best for them.

Don't lose sight of your goal to stay close and help the family pull together and love each other. Games will become a little more complicated, but play and have fun together.

FAMILY COUNCIL BLOOPERS

With kids, there are times in every family meeting where things don't go according to the plans laid out. Raising children is a task full of wonderful, unexpected twists, turns, and surprises. At times it's best just to go with the flow—whatever that may be. Pass the small stuff by and enjoy the journey.

Here are a few silly things that happened in our family councils:

When things got too quiet at our meetings—everyone was paying attention and absorbed in the discussion—our dog would nuzzle her nose under the area rug in the middle of the living room, make her little "comfort growl," and scratch her back, completely disturbing the meeting and taking everyone off task.

One Christmas day, when we had just enjoyed a spiritual family council, our dog slunk into the room with red fuzz and chocolate on her muzzle. The kids scurried around to find that she'd chewed a hole in the toe of a Christmas sock, eaten half the apple nestled there, and peeled the tinfoil off several chocolate kisses before she ate them and came to confess her guilt.

Our youngest daughter rushed into the house just as we started one family council meeting to tell us someone had smashed the window of her brother's truck and taken his stereo. We spent that family meeting in life experience—how to call the police and the insurance adjuster.

When the kids were young and we were reading together, one of them would invariably cross their eyes at another, stick out their tongue, or make any number of silly gestures to get everyone laughing.

Dad could also crack a joke and get everyone chuckling—just for fun.

CHAPTER 2:

Teaching Your Children through Family Councils

❧ Basic Principles ❧ to Teach

Belief System

Sit down with the other adults in your household and decide what you stand for. What moral concepts do you want to exemplify in your home? What about other values, like faith and trust? Do you live your life according to the things you want to teach?

Family councils are a great place to talk about how you look at life—a venue for discussions about values and convictions. Family councils can be a time to plan and put your belief system into practice to help your children internalize your standards.

Here are some examples of things to teach in formal family councils and informal settings:

> ✱ A child can learn about love. "If I've had a hard day where things haven't gone right, I know you'll be there with a hug and a listening ear."

* A child can learn trust. "If I need some advice about a friend, I know you'll help me decide what to do."
* A child can learn from his mistakes. "If I don't clean my bedroom well, I'll have to do it again."
* A child can learn to say "I'm sorry." "If I've taken my brother's baseball mitt and lost it, I need to say 'I'm sorry,' and buy a new one."
* A child can learn responsibility. "If I don't make my lunch for school, I will go hungry."
* A child can earn privileges. "I have a list of responsibilities equal to my list of privileges. If I accomplish my obligations, I will have additional opportunities."

RESPECT

The following family incidents could be handled as they happen, and many families work this way. However, there is an underlying lack of respect of individual boundaries that this family needs to address. If this is the case in your family, it's good to discuss these situations as a group and decide on some general rules.

The family is the place for children to learn to care for their own things and respect each other.

Lon, age 5, put his name on the agenda because he was tired of his three-year-old brother, Tyler, knocking down his block tower. Lon explained his problem at family council. Sarah, age 12, interrupted Lon to say that Heidi, age 14, kept borrowing her new shoes without asking.

Heidi, who was conducting the meeting, reminded Sarah about the non-interrupting rule and said she would have to wait while Lon had his turn. Then she could be next when all the agenda business was finished.

Tyler stood up, faced Lon, and put his hands on his hips. "You don't let me play."

Lon rose to his feet and glared at Tyler. "Yes, I do!"

"Let's not start the blame game." Dad stepped in between the boys and put a hand on each one's shoulder. "Let's talk about respecting each other's personal space and property."

"Fine," Lon huffed.

Sarah said that was her problem, too. She wanted her things respected.

Tom, age 17, suggested Lon include Tyler in making the block towers.

"Yes," said Tyler. "I want to play blocks with Lon."

"Okay," said Lon, "if you don't knock my building down."

Mom reinforced the idea of working together. She knelt down by Tyler to meet him eye-to-eye and asked him, "What are you going to do next time you play with Lon and the blocks?"

Tyler said, "I don't know." (This is what most kids say when asked this question.)

Mother looked at Tyler. "Will you help Lon build a tower?"

"Yes," said Tyler.

Mother asked again until Tyler could say, "I'll help Lon build the tower."

This process took a little time, but it helped Tyler clarify the message so he knew exactly what was expected of him.

Now it was the girls' turn.

Sarah suggested that maybe she and Heidi could ask before borrowing. If Heidi wore her shoes, then maybe she could put on Heidi's new scarf. Heidi agreed.

Dad cleared his throat. "It seems to me that you have all decided that it's better to work together and show respect."

"What are we voting on?" asked Sarah.

"I propose we ask for what we want," said Heidi. "I'll try to do better."

Everyone voted in the affirmative. This family may need to revisit the issue in another council if things don't run smoothly. Sometimes it takes a few tries before things iron out.

Dad could have launched into a lecture on respecting each other's property, but everyone seemed to understand the concept, so he let it go.

You notice there were no consequences established for if the children didn't show respect. A family could talk about this if getting in each other's space continued to be a problem. In our family, a much better reminder for the kids was to set up some kind of positive token economy when they remembered to be respectful.

A token economy (discussed later in Chapter 5) means that everyone puts a bean (or coin or pompom ball) in a jar when they are respectful (or for any other positive behavior the family decides on). Then the family plans a fun activity (let them choose by vote), like bowling or a trip to the zoo, when they have earned enough beans.

> ## "Men are respectable only as they respect."
>
> —RALPH WALDO EMERSON

HONESTY

Teaching children about honesty is an ongoing process that is best taught as an incident occurs. Each child will be a little different; help them understand accountability according to their age and level of sophistication. Look at your own patterns of honesty. Your children will follow your example.

Tony, age 7, really wanted a new Lego set. His friend Bill got Star Wars Legos for his birthday, and Tony knew if he and Bill each had sets, they could build twice as many space ships.

Tony knew his big sister, Ellen, had money in her piggy bank—a lot of money. Tony took Ellen's money without asking so he could buy the set. He could pay it back with his allowance, and he'd try to remember to do extra jobs so he could replace the money before Ellen knew it was gone.

He left the new Lego set over at Bill's house so his family wouldn't find out what he'd done.

In the meantime, Ellen went to the mall with a friend and found a new skirt she just had to have. When she came home to get her money, it wasn't there. She ranted and raved around the house. Tony kept quiet, and no one knew what had happened.

Tony hoped Ellen would forget about her money being gone. He watched Ellen put her name on the agenda for family council, and he knew he was in trouble. He wasn't hungry for dinner that night or the next. Mother asked if he was sick. He told her he wasn't.

At family council, Ellen explained her problem. Everyone already knew about it because she had been so upset. Tony sat there with his head down.

Father asked if he knew anything about the missing money. Tony started to cry.

Mother hugged him. "What's wrong?"

Tony told the whole story.

Ellen pressed her lips into a thin line and clenched her fists.

Mother told her to take a deep breath.

"How are we going to solve this problem?" asked Father.

"I'll pay the money back," said Tony.

"With interest." Ellen huffed. "If you borrowed from the bank, you'd have to pay interest."

Tony didn't know what to say.

At this point, the family could handle the situation several ways:

* Tony and Ellen could work the problem out between themselves outside of the council. (This method allows the children practice in negotiating and problem-solving. However, this may not be a good idea until Ellen has cooled off a little more.)

✳ The council could weigh in on the matter and vote as a family. (Since this procedure involves the entire family, it may facilitate important teaching moments for all the children.)

✳ The parents could lend Tony the money to pay Ellen and be the banker for him while he earns the money. (This allows Ellen to have her money immediately and gives the parents a chance to teach Tony about hard work and honesty.)

Whichever method the family chooses, the principle of family trust should be discussed. Ellen feels somewhat violated and suspicious that Tony is really sorry.

This is an important time for Tony. He can learn a lot from this mistake. He will probably remember this lesson in honesty and trust the rest of his life. Hopefully the parents will handle it in a positive way.

There's also something for Ellen to learn in all this. Can she cool off and then share her feelings in a kind and respectful way? She has every right to be upset, but she'll probably be able to think of a better solution and follow-through if she's calm.

This is a time when the basic theme of this family concerning trust will be developed. However you decide to handle an incident like this, make sure everyone in the family knows this is a safe place where trust is a priority.

> "As soon as you trust yourself,
> you will know how to live."
>
> —JOHANN WOLFGANG VON GOETHE

WORK ETHIC

Every household will run more smoothly if each member is part of the functioning whole. A child's self-esteem is built through love, kind words, *and* hard work. Industry will carry him or her toward his or her goals in life—whatever they are. Arm your kids with the gift of diligence.

One universal rule in our home was the fact that the chore chart needed to be changed about once a year—sometimes more often. It was lots of fun to meet in family council and watch the children devise a new plan for house and yard upkeep. Then off we would go with a new method and renewed vigor concerning our duties. There are several phone apps that will help with this. They're fun for the kids and help them set and keep track of their progress toward their goals.

Every family has a different task-completion pattern. With some families, there is a need for excitement, and they work really hard at the last minute to accomplish their goals. Others may work steadily along at daily intervals. Whatever your family arrangement is, teach your children to work.

Even though you raise your children in the same home, they have different personalities. Some of them have more energy than others. Some of them are more goal-oriented than others. Some are easy going. It would be very dull if we were all the same.

Whatever the child's personality, teaching a strong work ethic is important.

How do you help a child develop a work ethic?

One morning, I went upstairs to our teenage girls' bedroom. Clothes littered the floor. A wet towel decorated the pillow of an unmade bed. As I looked at the mess, I thought, what am I teaching these children?

I put my name on the agenda for family council.

When the chairperson called my name, I shared my frustration and asked, "What kind of a standard am I setting? What am I teaching you?"

Both girls looked at me and reminded me that they had studied late the night before for finals and had gone to a religious study group early the next morning before school.

I quickly backed off and apologized. "I can see that you have learned to study hard so you can do well on your exams, and you are keeping the religious commitment important to our family."

They cleaned their room the next Saturday.

These girls are grown now. One of them keeps a clean house. The other doesn't feel it's a priority. But both have excelled in their education, are great mothers, and are teaching the values important to our family.

This was the lesson our children taught me that family council:

Look at the big picture, and love me for who I am becoming.

Tim and Jennifer had been married for six weeks. It was the second marriage for both of them, and they each brought three children to the relationship. Tim's first wife had been ill with cancer for several years before she died. Their three children had learned to take care of themselves, do the dishes, the laundry, and clean.

Jennifer's ex-husband was an alcoholic and never helped with the housework. Jennifer asked the children to help her, but they complained that Dad never did any jobs so they shouldn't have to either. Jennifer did it all to keep the peace.

When Tim and Jennifer joined their households, Tim's children helped cook the meals and kept their rooms clean. They complained that Jennifer's kids didn't do anything. Although the kids were friends before the marriage, they now became irritated with each other.

Tim and Jennifer could see the tension increasing in their family and knew there was trouble ahead if they didn't do something. Jennifer had a friend that held family councils in her home each week and suggested that Jennifer and Tim try one to see if it could help their situation.

The meeting began with compliments. Tim's children had no

problem with saying nice things about everyone, but Jennifer's children felt uncomfortable doing it.

When they discussed the weekly responsibilities, tension grew high. The conference turned into a blame game.

Tim tried to diffuse it by saying, "The purpose of meeting together is to find a way to work with each other."

The defensiveness on the part of Jennifer's children continued.

Finally Jennifer stood. "We have to find some way to compromise on this." She looked at her children. "When we lived with your dad, I did all the work. We can't exist that way now. If you guys don't change your attitudes, you'll have a hard time keeping a job when you get older. We all have to help with the work."

Her children quieted.

Why did it help for Jennifer to say something? Why didn't Jennifer's kids listen when Tim said something?

If your relationship with a child is strong, he will listen to what you have to say. If there's no rapport, he won't respond.

Rules without relationships don't work.

Jennifer has a relationship with her children, so they will listen to her.

In my counseling practice, I found this situation so often in blended families. In many cases the family didn't come to me until a definite rift among members had formed from a dad trying to discipline a mom's children or a mom trying to discipline a dad's children.

Build the relationship first—then the kids will listen.

With some work, the Wilson family brainstormed job distribution and decided on the type of work chart they wanted. Tim suggested that they set up three teams, each consisting of one of Tim's children and one of Jennifer's children.

During the first week, Tim's children carried most of the workload, and Jennifer filled in and finished her kids' jobs. Then she complained to her children that they weren't pulling their weight.

Her oldest boy said to her, "Mom, you didn't make us work when we lived with Dad. So why do we have to work now? If we leave things, you'll finish them for us."

Jennifer looked at her son, stunned. He was right. If they left their jobs, she would finish them. She later told Tim, "I guess I did that so their dad wouldn't get mad."

Jennifer said she needed a therapist to help her sort through her feelings, so she made an appointment with me. Besides her therapy sessions, I recommended she and Tim attend a parenting class given at the community college.

Progress was slow, but Jennifer and Tim continued their family councils. Jennifer and Tim spent time with the children each day, listening to their successes and their problems. Jennifer learned to allow her kids the consequences of not getting their work done.

For instance, everyone voted at family council to clean up their after-school snacks before dinner. Several nights Jennifer found snack dishes all over the kitchen. She didn't fix dinner until the kitchen was clean. Through counseling and parenting classes, Jennifer gained strength. Her kids soon caught on that when a vote was taken at family council, their mother would follow through.

It's been several years since I saw the Wilson family. The children are all grown, but a Christmas letter from Jennifer let me know that everybody in the family works together now and they all get along.

Build on children's strengths. Find the good things they do or catch them in a moment of hard work and ask them if they feel good about what they're doing. Tell them how much you appreciate their help, but be sure to help them see the goodness in themselves so the children will become inner-directed.

Try saying, "I'll bet you feel good about the hard work you've done" or "How does that make you feel?"

Your words are not enough to build good feelings in a child. Your words will help make this happen, but words are not enough.

Children won't have good self-esteem until they act. Then they will know they are hard workers and that they are doing a great job.

Young children are naturally hard workers. Sometimes their hard work goes astray, and redirecting is a great technique to keep things functioning smoothly. If a two-year-old is cleaning the bathroom mirror with glass cleaner and is using half the bottle, help him see that just a squirt or two is enough. After he finishes his work, he can squirt all he wants with a spray bottle filled with water on the back patio cement.

We have to teach children by our own examples of hard work. And none of us learn something perfectly the first time. We need to practice over and over.

> "None of my inventions came by accident. I see a worthwhile need to be met, and I make trial after trial until it comes."
>
> —THOMAS A. EDISON

Setting and Following Up on Family Rules
Set Family Rules

Decide how you want to structure your family rules.

Some families like to plan ahead and have things organized, so they determine the rules ahead of time to ward off trouble before it happens.

Others don't feel it's necessary to set rules they may never use. They like working together and establishing them when the necessity arises. Such families are more casual in their way of handling life.

There is no right or wrong here. We all do things a little differently. Decide what will work best for you.

You can . . .

* Set the rules ahead of time to avoid trouble
* Set the rules as problems happen
* Set some general guidelines as a family and then deal with specifics as they come to the forefront

Reflect on the tenor of your home and decide what kind of a feeling you want to establish. Ask the children how they would like the family to function. They usually come up with great ideas. Then work together and institute the kind of relationships you want to foster.

Here's how a "plan ahead" family does it:

The Gordon family had a long-established rule about going to friends' parties on Sunday. Mom and Dad decided Sunday was a family day at the beginning of their marriage. The older boys never questioned the rule. But Sally, age 11, loved to do things with her peers. Her best friend Melissa's family had a boat. They often went to the lake on Saturday, but this upcoming weekend was special because it was Melissa's birthday. They planned a boating party for the whole weekend. Melissa invited Sally to go along. Sally thought about talking to her parents first to ask if she could go, but she figured they would say no. So she decided to put her name on the agenda for family council. Surely her three big brothers, who liked to water ski themselves, would support her in a weekend at the lake.

At family council, Sally explained her problem. She knew the family rule about Sunday, but just this once she wanted to go for the entire weekend. After all, it was Melissa's birthday, and Sally didn't want to miss it.

Her older brother Dan, age 17, said this was a problem for Sally and their parents to handle. He didn't want to be involved in this decision. Don, age 15, said Sally needed to be with the family on Sunday. She should stay home.

Sally's brother Tim, age 14, reminded everyone of the time Uncle Joe and his new fiancé had come for Sunday dinner. Tim left without his parents' permission and went to his friend's while the adults discussed the upcoming election in the living room. "I felt guilty the whole time I was gone. And besides, my friend's family had company over just like we did, and I felt very uncomfortable being there."

Father asked Sally, "Did you bring this request to family council thinking the boys would overturn our rule and vote to let you go?"

Sally hung her head. "Yes."

Father took her hands in his. "The purpose of family council is to help the family work together, not break the rules."

Tim shook his head. "You'll feel guilty if you go."

Sally glanced at Tim. "I probably will." She looked at her parents. "What will you do if I decide to go?"

Mother smiled and put her arm around Sally. "We don't want to make the decision for you. But remember, we're going to play that new game, Qwirkle, that Tim got for his birthday, and Blink, which is so fast and so fun."

Dad shook his head and began to chuckle. "I was so slow the last time we played!"

Sally smiled.

"Then don't forget it's Grandpa Tom's birthday. We'll talk to him over Skype and sing 'Happy Birthday,'" said Dad.

"You can choose," said Mother. "And I hope you decide that Sunday is a family day for you."

Dad patted her back. "It's a tough decision, but I know you'll make the choice that is best for you."

The family went on with the rest of the council. Afterward, Sally asked Mom and Dad if she could go to the lake on Saturday, and if they would mind picking her up Saturday night.

Dad looked at Mom. "That would be fine with us," he said.

Notice how the council didn't interfere in a matter between one child and the parents. They held to their family standard, but they allowed Sally to make her own decision. This is wise parenting because the child learns to rely on him- or herself to make a good decision rather than having the parents determine the consequences. The child is learning to discipline himself or herself rather than have the parents lay down the law.

Since the rule was "family time on Sunday," and everyone knew it, the council didn't need to make a decision. The choice was up to the individual.

Note also that Sally was checking to see if there would be any consequences if she decided to go, and Mother just outlined what the family would do for the afternoon. Again, she left the decision to Sally.

The family example was set. Everyone in the family committed to spend the day together on Sunday. When Tim "broke the rules" and went to his friend's house, he felt guilty, and Sally noted that when making her own decision.

Children learn from our example more than from what we say.

Here is another example from a family I worked with in therapy (for reasons other than those in this example).

The Pierce family consisted of Dad and the kids: Josh, age 18; Sam, age 15; and Mary, age 12. They liked to live causally and take life as it came. At the last minute, the family was invited to go four-wheeling at a desert resort six hours south of their home for the weekend. The oldest son, Josh, had to work. He tried to get off, but the schedule was set, and he couldn't find anyone to trade with him.

Dad thought one last vacation was a great idea. It would be the final holiday of the summer before Josh went off to college.

They sat down together for a family council meeting to discuss the matter.

"Let's brainstorm all the options we can think of," said Josh, who was conducting. "I don't want to be left home alone."

Josh suggested they go canoeing on the river and camp at the state park near home. That way he could join them after work.

Sam said they could rent four-wheelers and go out in the hills about thirty miles west of town to camp. Then Josh could spend the late afternoons and nights with the family.

Mary still wanted to go to the desert resort. She really loved four-wheeling. "It's not fair. Josh has had more time with the family than I have because he's older. It's my time to have fun now."

Dad said he wanted the family to be together one last time before Josh left for college. They needed to come to a consensus.

Mary complained and wanted her way.

Josh told Mary they could go four-wheeling closer to home so he could come, too. "If you're willing to compromise, you can come visit me at college. I'll get tickets for the first gymnastics meet at the university, and we'll go together."

Mary said that would be fun. She accepted Josh's idea.

The family voted to go four-wheeling in the hills west of town.

The Pierce family had an unwritten code of togetherness. It wasn't necessary to formally write out the rules. As the baby of the family and the only girl, Mary was probably used to having to her own way. Dad asked that they work together and then let the kids decide. They came up with a better solution than he could have thought of on his own.

I included the example of the Pierce family because, if you asked them, I don't think they would look at this as an example of a rule. They just wanted to foster closeness and went about achieving their goal.

How are these families alike? How are they different?

Similarities:

* The Gordon family and the Pierce family both had a strong sense of family togetherness.
* In both situations, the children influenced each other in their decisions.
* Both families looked for consensus in their decision-making process.

Differences:

* Since the Gordon family had a rule in place, the decision was left to the individual whether to follow the family rule or not.
* In the Pierce family, there was no rule, so negotiation made an agreement possible.

Decide how you want your family to function and set goals to accomplish your ideals. Will things work out perfectly? Probably not. But in both situations the children will learn the lessons and values their family wants to teach.

> ## "We all live with the objective of being happy; our lives are all different yet the same."
>
> —*ANNE FRANK*

FOCUS ON THE SOLUTION

Children can be very good at distracting. They are able to start a blame game in the blink of an eye. One of the things family councils can teach children is to stay solution-focused. What a valuable tool this can be as they become adults! They will be great as chairmen of the board, team leaders, classroom managers, or teachers. I love sitting in a lecture where the speaker can field questions but keep the focus of his talk and not go off on tangents.

Here is one family's experience in focusing on the solution:

Miranda, age 8, put her name on the agenda for family council because she said it wasn't fair that Darin, age 17, had more computer time that she did. And he got on the computer just to play his games when the battery on his game system died.

As Mother, a single parent, conducted the meeting that day, Darin explained to Miranda that he was not playing his games; he was gathering material for a research paper for school.

"You were not," said Miranda. "I caught you twice yesterday playing games."

Darin clenched his fists. "I had research to do on my paper."

Mother could see the discussion heading toward a blame game and redirected the conversation. "How can we solve this problem?"

"I need my computer time for school projects," said Darin.

"I always get less time than Darin because he's older," complained Miranda. "Besides, you never give in to me. You always give him what he wants. You like him better than me."

Mother looked at Miranda, "I'm sorry you feel that way. You always have good suggestions for solving our problems. Your idea last week for keeping the dirty dishes out of our bedrooms worked great. Have you got any thoughts for solving this problem?"

Notice Mother did not engage in Miranda's pity party. "You always . . . you never" means Miranda is headed for a "sorry-for-myself" bash. Mother keeps the discussion solution-focused.

"Sometimes I want to play my games when Darin's on the computer," said Miranda.

"Okay, I'll only play my games on my game system," suggested Darin.

Mother could see that Darin probably was playing games on the computer. She didn't confront him because she knew better than to ask a child to incriminate himself. It wasn't necessary to blame Darin because he had already offered a solution so that Miranda could have her computer time. He wasn't perfect, but he was becoming a responsible person.

"That's a good idea," said Mother. "And remember, Miranda, you've almost got enough money saved for your own game system."

"I know," said Miranda. "But I might want to get those new boots we saw on sale."

(So a game system is not really that important to her. Mother notes that but doesn't say anything.)

"It's great you have enough money to decide," said Mother. "Do we need to assign certain times for each of you to use the computer?"

"No," said Darin. "I can get my homework done while she's at dance. After that I have to go to work anyway."

Miranda didn't offer any solutions for this problem because she probably needed a cooling-off period before she could be objective. Darin could have gotten heated up over the incident, but he let it go, showing his maturity. Mental high-five for him!

Mother could take time when she and Miranda were alone for Miranda to tell her specific examples of why she thinks Mother loves Darin more—if she saw further intimations that it even needed to be discussed at all. It would be good for Mother to ask for specifics in this situation. Sometimes kids are just whining, but sometimes they have real concerns that need to be addressed.

Listen, listen, listen.

FACILITATE SOLUTIONS

At times, families like the following one have a problem keeping the house picked up. Toys, boots, and backpacks thrown around can create an obstacle course of the worst kind. Family councils can facilitate the solution. Everyone gains when the following happens:

* The problem is defined.
* Solutions are given.
* The discussion is productive.
* A decision is made.
* Follow-through is accomplished.
* The problem is solved.

Darla stepped over a pile of boots and shoes by the back door. Her arms were full of groceries. "I could break my neck coming into this house."

"Oh, sorry, Mom." Garrett, age 15, got up from the computer where he was doing his homework. "Can I help carry the rest in?"

"Yes." Mom swiped a pile of crafting supplies to the side of the kitchen table and set her bags down. She kicked a backpack into the corner and shoved the boots and shoes behind the back door before she went out to the car to get more groceries.

Garrett went to the car to get the last load. He set his bags down in the kitchen.

Mom plopped into a chair. "Thanks for helping me. I'm going to put my name on the agenda for family council. This house is an accident waiting to happen. Someone could really get hurt—even break a leg." She shoved Damon's snowboard from the middle of the kitchen to the side of the dishwasher.

Garrett laughed and rolled his eyes. "My friends will ask me if I broke my leg snowboarding, and I'll say, 'Yes. I tripped over the board in the middle of the kitchen.'"

They both chuckled.

"It's not funny," said Mom. "I'm an old lady. It could really happen to me."

Garrett smiled. "Put your name on the agenda, and go for the jugular." He went back to his homework.

At family council two days later, Mom explained her problem. "I don't know what to do. The house is a mess. I would never invite a friend over. And we could get seriously injured in the middle of the night if there were an emergency." Mom looked around the room. "The real problem is there are no girls but me in this family, and the male gender doesn't seem to care about cleanliness."

"Now that's not entirely true," said Dad.

"But the boys don't care," said Mom.

Garrett, Damon, age 12, and Seth, age 8, stared at the floor.

"It's true," said Damon. "My friends couldn't care less what our house looks like."

"I just play outside," said Seth. "It doesn't bother me."

"So nobody cares but me," said Mom.

Dad put his hand on Mom's shoulder. "I care because you care."

Mom smiled. "Thanks for that, but we're still outnumbered on the vote."

"We haven't voted yet," said Dad. "Let's brainstorm solutions."

Here's what they came up with:

"You could ground us if we don't pick up," said Damon.

"You know we don't do grounding," said Dad.

"How about charging us from our allowance if we don't pick up?" said Garrett.

"Just pick everything up and put it in a box in the garage," said Dad.

"That's sounding very good to me," said Mom.

"No TV or computer privileges until the house is clean," said Garrett.

"No," said Seth. "I don't want my games taken away."

"Then pick up," said Garrett.

"Just dump everything in our bedrooms if we don't clean up," said Seth.

"Don't touch my bedroom," said Damon.

"We'll just check the common rooms of the house," said Dad.

Mom cocked her head. "Common rooms for now."

"I still like the box in the garage," said Dad.

"We'll do it every night," said Mom.

"Who is going to pick it all up?" asked Damon.

"Let's rotate the job," said Mom.

"I don't want my stuff gone for good," said Seth.

"You could buy it back for a nickel a piece," said Garrett.

"How about a dime?" said Dad. "We'll use the money for a pizza party."

"So what I'm hearing," said Mom, "is that the person in charge each night will pick up everything in the common rooms of the house and put them in a box in the garage."

"And if you want the items back, you have to buy them for a dime each," said Dad. "Everyone in favor?"

Everyone voted for the nightly cleaning.

"Let's start the cleanup with the oldest person, rotate down to the youngest, and start over," said Dad. "My turn tonight—will seven o'clock be OK?"

They could have voted on the time, too, but everyone went with Dad's suggestion. The kids scurried to pick everything up and toss it into their bedrooms that night, so Dad didn't collect much—only an odd toy or two.

The next night, Mom got a full box. Dad forgot to put his sport jacket away, and Mom also found a tie behind the couch. Mom had to put her running shoes in the box, and the boys left coats, boots, and backpacks around.

Seth had to buy his backpack so he could do his homework, and the next morning he had to buy his boots for school. "My money is going down."

They had enough for a pizza party by the end of the week.

"This can be a Friday night treat each week," said Mom. "And I won't have to cook."

"But I have no allowance left," said Damon. "I wanted a new game for my game system."

Seth had to buy his homework twice that week and his backpack once.

Damon bought his snowboard four times.

"Keep it on the back patio," said Garrett.

"It's too expensive for that. Someone might take it." Damon put it in his bedroom.

Mom and Dad were surprised at how many things they lost to the garage box. Seth lost a couple of shirts he didn't like anyway, so he never bought them back.

Slowly, the family began to pick up after themselves, and Mom had friends over for lunch.

When we instituted this pickup system in our home, we called it the "Clutter Hunt." My husband and I lost a few things—like glasses, shoes, and my Bible, among other things—before we remembered to pick up after ourselves. The Clutter Hunt held it all.

Notice that both parents and children had to be a little more responsible. Sometimes we, as parents, think the kids are the ones to blame, when, in actuality, we have the same issues they do. If a family is to become the best it can be, we all need to continue growing and changing.

> ## "Action is the foundational key to all success."
>
> *—Pablo Picasso*

COOPERATE

No matter the disposition of a family, we all experience consequences of our actions. Parents do children a disservice if they don't allow them to take care of their own problems. The meting out of consequences can be given in either a spirit of cooperation or a spirit of punishment. There can be a subtle difference in the way we as parents handle situations. We can turn consequences into punishment if we're not careful.

If we are hard on ourselves, blame ourselves, and chide ourselves over our mistakes, we will probably do the same thing to our children. So, as we start to set our goals, we need to look at the direction we want our family to go and check out the way we treat ourselves. If we are kind and gentle with ourselves, we will do the same for our children.

> ## "Three things in human life are important. The first is to be kind. The second is to be kind. And the third is to be kind."
>
> *—Henry James*

Family council is a great place for the family to decide how to handle consequences with a spirit of cooperation.

A mother and her son, John, argued every day. John repeatedly forgot to take his backpack, with homework and lunch, to school. Mother, though irritated, dutifully ran it to school each day. When she picked John up after school, she felt angry because her day had been interrupted. She berated him for his forgetfulness. They both ended up in a bad mood for the afternoon. The other kids complained that Mother was always upset after school.

Mother put her name on the family council agenda. She hated being angry all the time.

John happened to be conducting family council that day. He asked Mother to talk about her problem, and then he shared his frustration. Other issues of forgetfulness came into the family conversation. John's teenage sister, Sally, forgot she had to make cookies for a party, and Dad had to run her to the store for chocolate chips. Vanessa, age , left her trike out in the rain, and it ruined the crepe paper decoration she had put on it.

John told Sally and Vanessa he was glad others besides him forgot things. Dad reminded the girls that this was a time to talk about John and Mother's difficulty. They could discuss their forgetfulness another time.

It would get too complicated to try to solve several people's problems at the same time, even though they were related. The family may decide a general rule about forgetfulness. But for now they needed to solve the situation on the agenda only.

"How should we solve this problem?" John asked.

"I'll help you make your lunch every evening," said Sally. "When I fix my own and pack all my favorite foods, I remember it the next day.

"You could write a reminder on the white board to jog your memory," said Mother.

"I never look at the white board," said John.

"Put your backpack by your shoes," said Dad. "I know you won't leave without them."

"Mother," said Sally, "I don't think you should take the pack to school because it puts you in a bad mood, and we all have to suffer for it."

"I'll try to remember my pack," said John, "but if I forget, I still want Mother to bring it to me."

Vanessa stood up. "My crepe paper is all gone. I need some more for my trike."

Dad put his arm around Vanessa and whispered, "Let's discuss this later. I'll help you."

Mother glanced at Vanessa. "We need a family rule about forgetfulness. Let's think about it for next week."

Dad rubbed his hands together. "I just gave a presentation on employee relationships last week. Two of the principles I taught were, 'Don't do someone else's job. Don't say yes when you mean no.'"

He suggested Mother try it.

Mother liked that idea and told the family it made her upset to have to do things the children could do for themselves. She would work on allowing them to be more accountable.

John said he would like to make his lunch with Sally every night, and he would put his pack by his shoes near the back door so he wouldn't forget it.

Mother said she wanted to be happy with John, but she couldn't if she had to run his backpack to school every day. She told John she wouldn't bring it to him anymore. Since John and Mother solved their problem through the discussion, no vote on the specific issue was necessary. Father said he appreciated all the cooperation in the family.

John wondered, since they were talking about cooperation, if Sally would make sure he had his backpack every day when Mother drove them to school.

Sally said that wasn't cooperating. That was taking over where

Mother left off. She told them she had been learning the difference between cooperation and rescuing in her child development class at school. Cooperation is working with someone. Rescuing is doing something for someone they can do for themselves.

After the discussion, John decided he was responsible enough to remember his own pack.

John forgot his pack the next day. He was starving because he'd had no lunch, and he had make-up work to do that afternoon because he didn't have his homework at school.

When they got home, Mother gave John a hug and a kiss. She took time to sit with him and ask about his day while he ate his lunch even though he was angry with her for not bringing his backpack to him. She told him she could see he was upset, and she was sorry he hadn't remembered his things. Hopefully tomorrow he would.

John needed peace and quiet while he got his homework done, so Mother told Vanessa to play dolls with her friends on the back patio. John remembered his backpack for a whole week before he forgot again.

Mother was happy when she picked John up after school each day, and John said he knew he was growing up because he remembered his lunch and his backpack. Mother allowed John to be responsible for his actions, and he learned to care for himself—a win-win situation.

John wasn't perfect at remembering at first, but he did become more responsible.

> "Help people become more motivated by guiding them to the source of their own power."
>
> —PAUL G. THOMAS

TEACH CONSEQUENCES

Consequences are part of everyone's daily lives. There are ramifications to everything we do. Every family has to come to grips with how much or how little they will support children as they learn to get along in the world. Will parents shore up children until they can paddle on their own, or will they allow children to learn to care for themselves when problems arise? There are pros and cons for both. Decide what works best for you and your family, and set your goals accordingly.

This family came for counseling on another matter, but the following "consequence" incident presented itself along the way.

It was early spring, and Sophia, age 7, loved to play in the slick, wet snow in the backyard. The melting snow made the sliding hill perfect. Bundled in her warm snowsuit, she started her run at the top—sometimes sitting down and sometimes flopped on her tummy—and glided all the way to the bottom where her boots hit a puddle and splashed mud in all directions, "making the snow look like a chocolate sundae," she said.

Every day after school, Sophia slid on the hill, and every evening her mother washed her muddy snowsuit so it would be dry for school the next day. Soon her mother got tired of the extra work and put her own name on the agenda for family council.

"How can we solve this problem?" asked Mother. "I already have enough washing with the twins still crawling all over the floor."

"I'll be in charge of cleaning Sophia's snowsuit," volunteered Father. "The hill looks like so much fun."

Sophia smiled up at her father. "Thank you."

"Fine by me," said Mother.

And for the next week Father tried to remember to wash her snowsuit, but he had to work late one night and had a scout meeting another night. A third night, he just forgot.

Sophia didn't like to wear a dirty snowsuit to school, so she put her name on the agenda.

"I'm sorry," said Father at the next meeting. "This has been a busy week. I'll try to remember for next week."

Sophia said she loved to play in the snow, but she didn't want to wear a muddy snowsuit to school.

Mother rearranged the toys on the floor for the twins and looked at Sophia. "How about you wash your own snowsuit? That way your father and I won't have an extra job, and you can play outside as often as you want."

"Great," said Sophia.

Mother showed her how to run the washer and how much soap to put in.

The next afternoon, Sophia played in the snow and the mud. When she came in, she started the washer and put her snowsuit in. But the family went out to dinner that night, and she forgot to put it in the dryer. The next morning her suit was still wet. She put it in the dryer but had to wear an old coat to school. She didn't forget again.

Note that neither of the parents scolded or shamed Sophia for getting dirty. They allowed the consequences to take their natural course. Father tried to rescue Sophia by doing the work for her, but he didn't have time.

As I counseled with this family, I encouraged Father to stand by Mother's decision and not do for Sophia what she could do for herself. The couple completed their goals in therapy, and I didn't see them again. I hope they stood together in letting Sophia solve problems for herself.

This family could have solved the snowsuit problem in an informal meeting since they only have one child old enough to understand the process, but they decided they would start having councils with Sophia even though the twins were still too small to know what was going on. When the children grew older, the solution system would already be in place, and the family would have an established means of running things smoothly.

Here's a family that handled consequences a little differently.

The Dolman family relocated to a small city in the hill country of Italy for a year to facilitate Dad's research for his company. They rented an old farmhouse in the vineyards near his work, enjoying the ambience this new adventure afforded.

The main problem the family encountered was school attendance for Tony, Regina, and Milly, ages 12, 10, and 8. They lived too far away to attend the nearest international school, and the children spoke no Italian, so they would have trouble attending the local school.

The family counseled concerning this problem, and everyone voted for homeschool. Mom ordered the materials and set up online classroom discussions for the children. They each had their laptops and were ready to start. They were to check in online every two weeks to make sure their work was completed.

However, as the family examined the new countryside, the children found more interesting things to do than school. Tony explored the Etruscan caves and learned all he could about the ancient civilization. He begged his mother to take him to see the caverns and paintings in other areas. He fell behind in his schooling. Regina slipped away as often as she could to help her father with his research. The study of soils and plants in the vineyards fascinated her. She became so focused on the local area that she didn't get her schoolwork done. Milly loved the Saint Bernard that belonged to the landowner. The dog came every day, and they explored the hills. Milly didn't give school a second thought.

After the first few days, Mom decided to check on the homework to see how the kids were doing. Very few assignments had been completed. She called an emergency family meeting after dinner to discuss the problem.

The Dolman children had been very busy studying things pertaining to their new culture and new life. Both Mom and Dad agreed that this was important. The family could take a field trip to visit other Etruscan caves because Tony was interested. This would be great for the whole family. Regina could continue to work with her father's research team. She loved being with his staff and followed their directions to the letter. Milly's love for the Saint Bernard was fine, Dad agreed, as long as they didn't have to feed the animal.

"But what about your schooling?" said Mom. "We're going back to the States in a year, and you don't want to get behind."

"But my science unit begins with photosynthesis," said Regina. "That's baby stuff compared with what Dad's doing here. I'll be fine when I get back home."

"You have to complete your math and English. Plus, your spelling needs some help," said Mom. "You can each do an extra unit on the things you are interested in, but you have to complete the home study course."

All three kids groaned.

"Work before play," said Dad.

"You mean dull work before interesting work," said Tony.

"Fine," said Dad. "Call it whatever you want, but you have to do it."

The family brainstormed:

Milly suggested they do a little every day.

Tony wanted to do it at night after dinner.

Mother said that was a bad time. Everyone would be too tired to study.

Regina wanted to get it all done on Monday so she would have the rest of the week off.

Dad said that wasn't realistic.

Mother said they should study at home in the morning and then spend the afternoon with what interested them.

The family voted—each for his or her own suggestion.

"This isn't going to work," said Dad.

"Yes, it will," said Milly. "I'll change my mind and vote for Tony's suggestion to study after dinner."

"I will, too," said Regina.

Mom and Dad voted for the morning study suggestion.

"We've got no consensus," said Dad. "We have to table this until later when everyone's thought about it a little more."

"We can't just let it go," said Mother. "We have to start today to get the homework done."

"Fine," said Dad. "Let's go with the children's suggestion and see what happens."

For the next week, everyone tried to study at night. Milly fell asleep before she finished her studies three out of the five nights. Regina finished her assignments, but Mom made her do them again because her work was fast and sloppy. She missed some of the questions because she hadn't read them thoroughly. Tony didn't get his homework done because when he got online, he got sidetracked, studying Etruscan vase painting.

The family met a week later.

"How are we going to solve this problem?" asked Mom. "No one has finished their studies on this plan."

"I'm too tired to do it at night," said Milly. "I want to do it in the morning."

"Me, too," said Regina. "I hate thinking all day that I have to come home to homework. That makes the day not fun."

"I don't mind the nighttime," said Tony.

"But you haven't been getting your work done during that time," said Mom.

"I know." Tony hung his head and sighed," "I guess I'll vote for the morning, too."

"So, let's see," said Dad. "Everyone is voting to get their work done in the morning before they do other daily activities?"

"One section per day," said Mother.

"Yes," said the children together.

The problem was solved for the present.

The homeschool program failed in the beginning because of the following reasons:

* There was no set study plan.
* There was no parental involvement.
* The established goals were not specific enough.

Mom had to be more engaged in the study program. Now that goals were created with a set study plan, the family had a better chance of success.

Note also the wisdom of family consensus. Everyone needs to agree for a program to work. It's great that this family was secure enough and flexible enough to let the children try their plan and fail. For children to become internally-directed, they have to have a few try/fails in order to appreciate their successes.

> ## "You have to risk failure to succeed."
>
> —AN WANG

DON'T GIVE UP

As you sort through family problems, it may take a few family councils to get things running smoothly. Sometimes children learn best by trial and error. It's good for them to work together to figure things out. If Mom and Dad solve all the little malfunctions, kids won't learn.

Mom didn't like to cook in a messy kitchen. She put her name on the agenda, and the family voted to clean up their after-school snacks before Mom started dinner.

Kyler, age 16, walked in the door from soccer practice and threw his bag and books in his room. "It's six o'clock. I'm starving. What's for dinner?"

"Spaghetti and meatballs." Mom sat in the living room, curled up in the recliner and reading a book.

"Uh . . ." Tyler pointed toward the kitchen. "What time will it be ready?"

"As soon as the kids clean up their dishes." Mom went back to her book.

Moody, age 14, came down the hall. "Remember the family council. Mom won't fix dinner until everyone cleans up their snack dishes."

Kyler turned to Moody. "But I haven't had a snack, and I'm hungry for dinner."

"My dishes are cleaned up," said Moody. "Go talk to Eric and Carolyn."

"Hey, guys!" Kyler yelled toward the bedrooms. "Clean your dishes up so Mom will fix dinner."

"Fine!" Eric, age 12, trudged into the kitchen. "I hate cleaning up after myself."

"Do it anyway," said Kyler. "I'm starving. Where's Carolyn?"

Eric shrugged. "Playing Dress-the-Barbie on her iPad." He shook his head. "It's the stupidest game I ever saw."

"Carolyn." Kyler poked his head in her bedroom door. "Clean up your snack dishes so Mom will cook dinner."

"Just a minute." Carolyn, age 8, looked up. "I've almost got this whole outfit coordinated. Barbie's going on a cruise to the Caribbean."

Kyler rolled his eyes. "Oh, come on. I'm starving."

"I'm not hungry. I had the best cookies over at Megan's house today. Wish you could have had some."

"Figures," said Kyler.

"Meg and I are trading Barbie's clothes online." Carolyn went back to her computer.

Kyler grabbed a couple of apples from the fridge and stomped off to his room. "Hurry. I'm hungry."

Half an hour later, Kyler yelled to his sister again. "Carolyn, we're waiting."

Carolyn appeared in his doorway. "Sorry. I just lost track of time. I'm going to clean up right now."

Kyler got up from his desk and went to the living room to talk to Mom. "This isn't working."

"Put your name on the agenda and we'll talk about it tonight at family council," said Mom. "Carolyn's cleaning up now. I'll have dinner ready in a few minutes."

That night at the meeting, Kyler shared his feelings. "You guys all had snacks after school, and I didn't. I want dinner to be on time when I get home."

The family brainstormed.

"Take a snack to practice," said Moody.

"Nobody can leave the kitchen until they clean up," said Eric.

"Ditch the rule altogether," said Kyler. "It's dumb anyway."

"I can't fix dinner in a messy kitchen," said Mother. "If you want to cook dinner, you can."

"I'll clean up after my snack," said Carolyn.

"Any other ideas?" asked Dad.

No one had any more suggestions.

"I think there are some good ideas here," said Dad. "Kyler, you can take a snack with you to eat on the way home." Dad looked at the other kids. "Let's clean up right after you fix your snack."

"And I love the idea of someone else cooking dinner," said Mom.

After more discussion and voting, the family decided to do the following:

* If anyone had an after-school practice, they could take some granola bars to eat on the way home.
* Everyone would clean up right after fixing their snacks.
* Mom would have several quick-fix meals on hand so someone else could cook if they wanted to.

Maybe the problem was completely solved, and maybe it wasn't. The family may have needed another meeting if things didn't run smoothly. But they had the skills to solve the problem, even if it took a little time.

Notice how each one of the children was becoming more responsible for him- or herself and more involved in finding solutions.

Allowing children to solve their own problems has its inherent rewards. When a dispute concerns only the kids, Mom and Dad wisely let them find a solution together.

Eileen, age 13, and Dugan, age 15, shared a bathroom. They took turns cleaning it each week, but it was still messy. Eileen put her name on the agenda.

"I have a problem with the bathroom," she said. "Dugan's towel is always on the floor. I have to walk over it to get to the sink." She looked at Dugan. "I would hate to dry myself with a towel that had mopped the floor."

"Good thing you don't have to use it, then," said Dugan.

"I would be embarrassed to have my friends use our bathroom," said Eileen. "The toilet is never clean."

"Do we need to re-teach you how to scrub a toilet?" asked Dad.

"No," said Dugan. "I just hate doing it. Besides, it's OK because Eileen scrubs it every other week. That's good enough."

"Not if you miss," said Eileen.

Mom rolled her eyes. "Let's stick to the cleaning problem. How are we going to solve this?"

They all brainstormed.

"Dugan needs to make himself an outhouse like grandpa used to have on the farm," said Eileen, "and live outside."

"How about we hire a cleaning lady?" said Dugan.

"Who's paying?" Dad looked at Dugan.

"Don't look at me," said Dugan. "I don't have any money."

"I'll clean the bathroom every week, and he can trade me another job," said Eileen.

"Like what?" asked Dugan.

"Clean up my dinner dishes and load the dishwasher four nights a week."

"Four? That's too many," said Dugan. "Three."

"Done," said Eileen.

"Wait a minute," said Dad.

"Why wait?" said Mom. "They've decided, and it's their bathroom. Let's vote."

"I'll clean the bathroom every week," said Eileen, "and you can do my dishes Monday, Wednesday, and Friday."

Everyone voted for this plan.

"Now, what about your towel?" asked Eileen.

"I don't care if it's on the floor," said Dugan.

"But I care if my friends come over," said Eileen.

"Then you pick it up," said Dugan. "Throw it in my room."

"Fine, I will," said Eileen. "Then I know the bathroom will be clean."

Mom and Dad remained silent. They would give the decisions a week to see what happened.

Eileen threw Duncan's towel onto his bedroom floor. Duncan didn't like to walk over it, so he kicked it under the bed. When he got out of the shower the next morning, he didn't have a towel. He ran dripping to the bedroom and remembered he'd kicked his towel under the bed. He retrieved it, but it was covered with dust bunnies. He dried off with his sweatshirt. He washed his towel and hung it up from then on. He learned from natural consequences—at least for the time being.

Eileen scoured the bathroom, and Duncan cleaned up the dinner dishes on Monday and Wednesday. But by Friday, he was tired of doing his original job (setting the table and helping Mom get dinner on), and doing Eileen's job (clearing up dinner and loading the dishwasher).

"I don't like all this work," Duncan complained to Mom.

"Put your name on the agenda," said Mom.

Duncan did. He explained his problem and asked if Eileen would trade back.

"I don't know," said Eileen. "I like getting out of cleaning up after dinner."

"Please?" asked Duncan.

"How do I know you'll scrub well enough so the toilet doesn't stink?" asked Eileen.

Duncan shrugged. "I know how. I'll do a good job."

"Fine," said Eileen. "But if my friends come over and it's dirty, I want to trade back."

"Deal," said Duncan.

Mom and Dad allowed Eileen and Duncan to find their own resolution. Note that Duncan learned more from making his own choices than he would have if his parents had made him do it their way. Eileen was assertive enough not to let Duncan fall short of his responsibilities.

Sometimes staying out of children's problems is the best way to teach them.

❦ CHILDREN'S ISSUES ❦
NAME-CALLING

Children learn communication patterns from many different sources: home, extended family, school, community groups, and church organizations. Even if we, as parents, keep our family interaction positive, our children are exposed to name-calling and, at times, bullying. (See "Bullying" just following this section.)

It's important to let children know your interaction goals. If you want a loving, caring family, teach them that positive, uplifting communication leads to positive, uplifting relationships.

"You're fat," yelled Samantha, age 10, at her sister Bea, age 8.

"I am not!" Bea yelled back. "Your nose is crooked."

"What?" Sam ran to the bathroom to look in the mirror. "It is not." She stuck her tongue out at Bea.

Bea fell into Mother's arms. "Am I fat?"

"You're just the way you're supposed to be," said Mother.

Dad looked up from his newspaper. "You're wearing all Sam's hand-me-down clothes, so you must be about the same size she used to be."

Mother worried about the name-calling. What should she do?

Later that week, she went to lunch with a friend. "What's your advice?" she asked her friend.

"When my girls went through that phase, we talked about hurting each other's feelings. They were more sensitive after that. Kids have to figure out how to get along."

"But your girls are best friends," said Mother.

"They weren't always. They had to learn."

Mother put her name on the agenda for the next family council meeting. When it was her turn to share, the girls got defensive.

"I don't call Bea names," said Sam, "unless she does it first."

"No fair," said Bea. "That's not true."

Mother could see the blame game starting and redirected them back to the problem and the solution. "What are we going to do about this problem?"

"You are both good at giving compliments," said Dad. "How about you try to do that instead of name-calling?"

"I guess," said Bea.

The family voted to adopt Dad's idea. But during the week the girls fell back into the same pattern.

Mother put her name on the agenda again. "How are we going to solve this problem?"

"I don't know," said Sam. (A child's pat answer.)

"Me neither," said Bea.

"Dad and I will wait for you to think of something," said Mother.

Silence.

Mother looked at the girls. "While you're thinking, let me ask you a question. How does it make you feel, Bea, when Sam calls you fat?"

Bea studied her hands. "I feel bad—like maybe I am fat."

Sam sat up straight. "Well, I feel awful when you say my nose is crooked."

"Why do we try to make each other feel terrible?" asked Dad.

"I don't know," said Bea.

"I guess it's just a habit," said Sam. "A lot of the kids at school do it."

"How do you feel when it happens at school?" asked Mother.

"I get angry and don't want to play with those guys," said Sam.

"Sisters need to be friends," said Dad. "You need to learn how to get along with each other."

"What will help you remember to be nice to each other?" asked Mother.

Bea thought for a minute. "In Brownie Scouts we're earning a pizza party by being nice to each other. Every time we do a good deed, we put a smiley-face sticker on our chart. When we fill the whole page, we get a party."

"I like that idea," said Sam. "If we give each other a compliment, we can put a sticker on a chart." She turned to Bea. "We can make one together."

"Good idea," said Dad. "I'll get some stickers on the way home from work tomorrow."

"No," said Bea, "we want to pick them out."

Mother smiled and breathed a sigh of relief. "I'd love to take you to the store."

The girls didn't call each other any names the next week. They remembered to give each other compliments and got several stickers on the chart they made.

It takes at least six weeks to change a habit, so this may not have been the end of the problem. The girls could fall back into old patterns, but the family could continue to share their feelings and change the token economy if necessary.

If the parents are positive with each other in their interaction, the girls hopefully followed the same communication pattern. As Sam and Bea matured, the time came when the reward system wasn't needed any more. The girls internalized the family interface model, learned to empathize with each other, and required no incentive.

I love giving positive feedback to others because I feel good when I do it. If children can see how this affirmative communication cycle works and see the good feelings it engenders, they will want to be part of it too.

Sisters are like flowers in the garden of life.

BULLYING

Bullying is a universal problem. Many youth today are victimized by bullying. Fortunately, schools are beginning to address the problem. Units and lesson plans have been created to teach children about the following:

* The facts of bullying
* How to ask the bully to stop
* How to let adults know what's happening
* How to stand up for others who are being bullied
* How to develop good communication skills in relation to bullying

At home, parents and siblings can also be involved in teaching assertive principles at family council meetings. Most kids—if they haven't been bullied by the adults in the family—will respond positively to helping each other with social skills.

Let's see how one blended family solved the bullying problem.

Ethan, age 13, didn't like his new family. He and his dad had spent the last eight years alone together and had gotten along just fine. Now he had a new mother and a shrimpy little six-year-old brother, Alexander. The kid was skinny, wore glasses, and had straw-colored hair that stuck out in every direction. Shrimpy's mother should at least have called him "Alex" instead of "Alexander." Alex is a pretty cool name, Ethan thought.

Ethan knew Shrimpy was used to being picked on because all Ethan had to do was reach out with his fist like he was going to punch Shrimpy, and Shrimpy ducked.

Now, to make matters worse, Ethan had lost all his friends. His dad and stepmom had both sold their houses, and the family moved to a new location in a different school district, so Ethan had to find new guys to hang out with. Things were not looking good.

The first weeks of school went by, and Ethan found some boys his age who lived in the neighborhood. As they got off the bus and started toward home, Ethan could see Shrimpy across the street, walking home from the grade school with some bigger boys.

"Pest." A kid shoved Shrimpy.

"Four-eyes." Another boy reached out his foot to trip him.

Ethan ignored the little group on the other side of the street and concentrated on the guys he was with.

Jeremy, one of his new friends, walked next to Ethan, watching the boys across the street. "I hate to see bullying."

Another new friend, Robert, followed Jeremy's gaze to Shrimpy and his attackers. "We had a unit on bullying in Social Studies."

"We should stop them," said Jeremy.

Ethan took a deep breath. He'd had a unit about bullying in his old school, and, after all, Shrimpy was his brother. "I should stop them. Be back in a sec." He sprinted across the street. "Hey, what's up, bro?" He gave Shrimpy a high five.

Shrimpy looked up at Ethan in surprise.

"Want to walk home with me and my friends?" Ethan asked Shrimpy.

Shrimpy smiled. "Sure."

"Is this your brother, Shrimpy?" asked the boy who shoved Shrimpy.

"Yep." Shrimpy smiled.

"He's cool," said the kid who tried to trip Shrimpy.

The brothers sprinted back across the street.

Ethan looked at his new friends. "This is my brother, Alexander."

The boys high-fived Alexander.

Later that night, Ethan pulled his dad aside. "I think we need to teach Alexander how to stick up for himself."

"What do you mean?" asked Dad.

"Well, he walks with a slouch. And if anyone looks sideways at him, he ducks."

Dad put his hand on Ethan's shoulder. "Good point. Thanks for watching out for him."

Alexander's mother came into the room. "Private discussion?"

"No," said Dad. "Ethan just has some good ideas for our next family council. Maybe we can do some role-playing."

"About what?" she asked.

Ethan looked at his feet. How could he tell her that her son needed an overhaul? "Oh, just boy stuff."

"Boy stuff?" She studied Ethan. "Can't wait to hear it."

Ethan raised his head just in time to see Dad wink at him. Ethan imagined high-fiving Dad in his head. Ethan would think of some things to share with Alexander at the meeting.

Ethan found his old school notes about bullying and made a list of things to talk about.

* Stand up straight.
* Look at other kids when talking to them.
* Step out of the way if others try to trip or hit you.
* Smile and be friendly.

✳ If kids are teasing you, tell them to stop.

✳ If they don't stop, get an adult to help.

Two nights later at the family council meeting, it was Alexander's turn to conduct.

"I don't know what to do," said Alexander. "I've never conducted a meeting before."

"I'll help you." Ethan moved next to Alexander on the couch. "My name's first on the agenda anyway. And I need you to help me."

Ethan showed Alexander how to start the meeting. After compliments and work assignment changes, Alexander called on Ethan.

"I've got some boy stuff to talk about," said Ethan.

"Like what?" asked Alexander.

Ethan looked at Alexander's disheveled hair. "I just got a new jar of hair gel. I'll help you fix your hair with it." Ethan glanced around the room. His parents smiled.

Alexander looked up at Ethan. "Sure."

"We'll make your hair look real cool." Ethan took a deep breath. Now for the hard part, he thought. "Remember the other day when those boys were bullying you?"

Alexander hung his head. "Yeah."

"I have some ideas to help you take care of yourself."

"Like what?"

"How about you stand up straight?"

"Like this?" Alexander stood up and put his shoulders back.

"And look me in the eyes when you talk," said Ethan.

Alexander raised his head. "I can do that."

"Great," said Ethan. "Now, here's a tough one. If someone shoves your back, just step out of the way and grin at them."

"How?" asked Alexander.

"Like this." Ethan showed him.

"Let's all practice it," said Dad.

All four members of the family involved themselves in the role-play, and soon they were all laughing, missing punches, and stepping aside.

They talked about the other things on Ethan's list and then had brownies for dessert.

"Thanks," said Ethan's new mother. "You're a great big brother."

Ethan smiled. Maybe he would like this family after all.

All bullying situations won't fall into place like this one did. But it's great for the entire family to role-play being assertive at family council meetings. Children need to learn appropriate social skills, and parents and older siblings can be of great help working through problems.

> # "Just as hope rings through laughter, it can also shine through tears."
>
> —MAYA ANGELOU

COMMUNICATION TRIANGLES

The healthiest way to communicate with others is person-to-person. If I have a problem with someone, the best thing for me to do is talk with him or her and work out the trouble.

If I see a problem and I'm worried or afraid to talk to the person about it, then I feel tension. And, unfortunately, the most common way to release the tension is to talk to a third person about the problem—creating a triangle.

Junior high is the age of triangles. The "he saids" and "she saids" blaze through the halls and classrooms like wildfire. As we mature, we learn to talk to each other about our problems.

Family council is a good place to teach person-to-person communication skills. As families discuss worries and challenges in a personal setting, children learn to share feelings and stay solution-focused.

Georgia, age 14, thought her little sister Belle, age 12, was way too friendly with the wrong kind of boys at school. Their cousins, Lulu and Ruby, ages 14 and 16, didn't go to the same school as Georgia and Belle, but they all went to church together.

One Sunday after their church meeting, Georgia told Lulu and Ruby all about Belle's behavior at the last basketball game. "You should have seen Belle. She was hanging out with the older boys my age who think they are cool and don't have to study. I have algebra with two of them, and they got Ds on their last tests. That kid with spiky hair, Sam, even had his arm around her."

Belle accidentally overheard some of this and slipped into a nearby classroom to listen.

When Georgia had finished, Belle began to cry. She was so angry that she came out of the room and confronted Georgia. Lulu and Ruby felt terrible and told Belle they were sorry she was upset.

On the way home from church, Belle was irritated at everyone. That evening, she went to her room and stayed there. She didn't come out for dinner. She walked to school the next day because she didn't want to ride in the same car with Georgia.

Belle told Mother after school, "I'm so upset at Georgia, I don't ever want to speak to her again."

Mother stroked Belle's arm. "Do you want to discuss it with Georgia when she gets home from play practice today, or would you like to talk about it at family council?"

Belle looked at Mother with tears in her eyes. "I don't want to talk to Georgia alone. I'll just cry and get angry."

"We can talk to her together you if you want," said Mother.

"I think family council is the best place," said Belle. "Then you and Dad will be there to help me if I can't think of what to say."

"Family council isn't for two days," said Mother. "Are you sure you want to wait that long?"

"Yes." Belle sighed.

For the next two days, Belle walked to school alone and didn't speak to Georgia.

The parents could have forced the girls to sit down and talk right after the incident happened, but they let them both cool off. Most importantly, Mother gave Belle her choice of how she wanted to handle the situation. There's a lot of trust in this family for Belle to decide family council was a safe place to discuss this sensitive issue.

The night of the council, the family sat at dinner. "I'm glad we have family council tonight. I don't like the tension we've had in the house," said Dad.

Belle shared her problem at the meeting that night. "Georgia, I can't believe you told my personal business to the world."

"It wasn't the world," said Georgia. "It was family."

"I can't ever trust you again," said Belle.

"I'm sorry," said Georgia. "I'm just worried about you. You were sitting with the wrong kind of boys."

"I don't like the nerds who study all the time like you do," said Belle. "I like the cooler kids. I want to play and have fun."

"Is it all right for us to be different and have individual likes and dislikes?" asked Father.

"I guess," said Georgia. "But those boys are not going to go to college."

"You don't know that," said Mother.

"That's right," said Belle. "I sat with Sam, and his father is a doctor."

Notice that there was some clarification going on here. The girls shared their thinking. Kids need to talk about who they are and what they think. But after the explanations were given, Dad returned the focus to the solution.

Dad put his hand on Belle's arm. "So how would you like to solve this problem?"

"I'd like to talk about our troubles here first before we tell the world."

Georgia sighed. "It wasn't the world. It was family."

"I don't care," said Belle.

You can see the conversation turning into a blame game.

"So what you're saying," Mother turned to Belle, "is that you'd like to talk things through in family council first."

Belle smiled. "Yes."

"Everyone in favor, say 'Aye,'" said Father.

The vote was unanimous.

"The greater issue for me," said Mother, "is that we trust each other. Trust has been broken here, and I'd like it not to happen again."

"So what are we going to do next time we have a problem?" asked Father.

"It isn't *we*," said Georgia, "it's *me*."

"No," said Mother. "This is about family boundaries, and we're all involved. Let's all remember to share things here first."

Georgia smiled and gave Belle a hug. Both girls giggled.

"We can do that," said Georgia.

Note the way Mother talked about family boundaries, making the entire family responsible to keep each other's trust. This helped Georgia to see that it wasn't just her problem. Everyone needs to respect each other enough to talk person-to-person about difficulties.

Give your kids the gift of positive one-on-one connections. It won't take away all your problems, but it will teach the family how to solve them.

The process of defining self is to define our values.

SIBLING COMPETITION

Competition is all around us. Our society is peppered with it. Everyone is trying to get ahead of everyone else. My preference is to see relationships in a more cooperative way. We don't have to have winners and losers. Everyone can win.

In families where siblings next to each other in the birth order are of the same sex, the competitive spirit can be especially heightened.

Kayla, age 7, practiced spelling her words with Mom. Avery, her little sister, age 5, sat on the bed and listened.

"Spell *new*," said Mother.

"N-e-w," spelled Kayla.

"Good," said Mother. "*Few*."

"F-e-w," spelled Kayla.

"*Blue*, the color," said Mother.

"B-l-e-w," spelled Kayla.

"No," said Avery. "That's like the wind blew. The color is b-l-u-e."

"What?" Mother looked at Avery. "How did you know that?"

Avery smiled. "Just listened when she went over her words before."

"I'm done practicing." Kayla picked up her doll and left the room.

Mother watched more carefully. Avery knew Kayla's math facts as well as Kayla did. Avery had begun reading Kayla's books.

"What should I do?" Mother asked Kayla's teacher. "I want Kayla to feel good about herself. She doesn't need a little sister that can do her schoolwork better than she can."

"Find something Kayla is good at and point out to the children that they each have talents. Their minds just work differently. One isn't better than the other. They are both good."

"I'll try it," said Mother.

The teacher smiled thoughtfully. "I've had siblings where the smartest child isn't always the best student. The more hardworking child can speed ahead of the smarter one."

Mother worried about how to approach the girls. What were Kayla's gifts? Kayla was wonderful with people. She loved everyone. But how could she point that out to Kayla?

That weekend, Aunt Josie and Uncle Michael came to visit. Kayla fussed over their new baby, cuddling and rocking him.

Avery watched Kayla for a few minutes and then went to find her stuffed animals. "I'm going to build a new world on a distant planet."

Mother linked her arm through Aunt Josie's. "Avery and her make-believe."

"Kayla's going to make a great babysitter," said Aunt Josie.

"Yes, she is."

Mother had her example for family council.

Mother put her name on the agenda for the next meeting. She explained that she was surprised when Avery could spell Kayla's spelling words. "We are all different," Mother continued. "Look at Daddy and me." She reached for her husband's hand. "He loves to read the newspaper and keep up on what's happening in the world around us."

"And you don't," said Avery. "You don't ever watch the news. You like to read those mushy churchy novels."

Mother laughed. "You don't miss a beat, Avery."

"You girls are different also," said Daddy. "One of you is totally into make-believe. Which one of you does that?"

"I do." Avery smiled.

Daddy continued. "One of you loves children and babies—especially Aunt Josie's."

Avery started to speak, but Mother put her hand up. "Let Kayla answer."

Kayla smiled. "That's me."

"Everyone is a little different," said Mother. "Isn't it great?"

"If we need a babysitter, Kayla can help us," said Mother.

"If we want an exciting story," said Daddy, "Avery's our girl."

Obviously, this didn't take care of the problem forever, but helping children to see their own talents and goals is important. Next time this family revisited this concept, they could augment the discussion with other talents each girl possesses.

Another dynamic I have observed over the years is that when children play together, they pick up strength from each other. If one child is a good dancer, the other child will learn. If the first child likes to ride bikes, the second will become better at riding also. Synergy in relationships will enhance both children's lives.

As a busy mom, I funneled all my girls into the same music lessons and the same sports. In retrospect, I would do that differently. I just heightened the competition by making everyone do similar activities.

Our oldest daughter has a good musical ear and can sit down at the piano and play almost anything without music. Our second daughter loved science and swimming. She enjoyed a hard workout after a day of study. She is a great organizer. Our third daughter is an excellent teacher and has loved children since she was little. Our fourth child is a literary buff—a voracious reader. Our fifth daughter is an artist. I have many beautiful pieces of her pottery in my house. Yet I tried to funnel all these girls into piano and swimming lessons. They survived in spite of me and have developed their own talents, and they have taught me many lessons along the way.

There are many ways to lessen this problem of competition in families. It's important to expose children to a wide variety of subjects and let their interests lead them—with parental support, of course.

Minimize the competition by doing these things:

* Share with each child their strengths and help them develop into their very best.
* Encourage each child to learn from siblings and friends.
* Allow each child to choose to develop their own talents.

Some may say competition is good for us. It makes us strong. Children will get plenty of competition along life's path. We don't have to always have winners and losers—especially at home. Everyone can win by being the best they can be.

> ## "The privilege of a lifetime is being who you are."
>
> —*Joseph Campbell*

Temper Tantrums in the Family

Anger episodes can disrupt a family, increase tension, and reduce the quality of life for the entire family. When a child is having a temper tantrum, it's a good idea to give them a cooling-off period somewhere. Many educators call it a time-out. The goal of this separation is to give the child a chance to change his or her thinking because our thinking determines our feelings. The other thing it does is give the angry child the signal that his deviant behavior doesn't have the power to disrupt everyone's life.

When a child is two, it's easy to pick him up and set him in time-out. As a child grows older, it becomes more difficult. Let's see how one family handled the temper tantrum problem with an older child.

Theresa and Glen had been married for three months. One of the problems the couple encountered in blending their family happened with Theresa's son, Wayne, age 6. He let his temper get the best of him whenever he didn't get his way.

One evening, the couple sat on the couch in their living room.

Wayne stormed into the room. "I can't find my new Lego set we bought at the store today."

"You took it to your bedroom when we got home," said Theresa.

"I can't find it!" Wayne threw himself on the floor, kicked, and screamed.

"How can I help?" asked Glen.

Theresa shrugged. "He's always been like this. His father said there was nothing we could do about it. He just has a bad temper." She got up and went to Wayne's bedroom and came back with the Lego set.

Wayne stopped screaming, grabbed the box, and ran to his room.

"I know this has to stop," said Theresa. "But I don't know what to do."

"I don't like him being rude to you, making you go get things," said Glen. "But I don't think he'll take any guidance from me right now."

"I wish I knew how to handle him," said Theresa.

Glen put his arm around Theresa. "When Connie was younger, we knew she needed some space if she began getting irritable. So she spent a little time in her bedroom with her dolls, and she would be fine later."

"Well, girls are easier than boys," said Theresa.

"Hey, what's up?" asked Tony, age 13, walking into the room.

"We're just talking about Wayne's temper," said Theresa.

"Oh, man, Connie was the worst," said Tony. "My parents used to put her in her bedroom and let her play until she got over it."

Connie, age 14, entered the room. "I heard that. Will I never live my temper down?"

"We're just saying what a great job you've done in conquering it," said Glen.

"Thanks," said Connie. "It was hard, but I feel good that I did it."

"I don't think Wayne can change," said Theresa. "His dad always told him he was bad because of his anger and that he could never get over his temper."

"That makes me feel terrible," said Connie. "I'm not bad because I had a temper. And he can get over it—I got over mine."

"Maybe you can tell him what it's been like for you," said Theresa.

"I'd love to." Connie twisted her hair around her fingers. "Can we do it at family council? I don't know what to say on my own."

"Sure thing," said Glen.

At the family meeting, Connie began to talk about how she had a bad temper and how she learned to control it.

Wayne watched her. He looked down at his hands and smiled.

Connie explained how she went to her room and played with her dolls when she was upset.

"How did that make you feel better?" asked Wayne.

"I thought about my dolls and not what made me angry," said Connie.

"Do you want to try that when you get upset?" Theresa asked Wayne.

Wayne went to sit on his mother's lap. "I guess."

"What will you do in the bedroom?" asked Connie. "I know you don't want to play with dolls."

Wayne laughed. "I'll play my game system or build my Legos."

"Good idea," said Connie.

A few days later, Wayne got angry because his favorite socks were in the dirty clothes. He lay on the living room floor, kicked, and screamed again. This time Theresa asked him to go to his room until he could be happy. He refused.

She looked at Glen. "What do we do now?"

Glen shrugged. "I don't know."

"Let's leave him alone in here," said Connie.

Theresa shook her head. "How will that help?"

"I don't know," said Glen. "Let's try it."

Glen and Theresa walked down the hall to their room.

Wayne stopped and looked around. He ran to his mother's door and pounded on it.

"This isn't working," said Theresa as she opened the door. Wayne immediately lay down on the floor, kicked, and screamed again.

Later that week, Theresa called and made an appointment to come to my office to discuss Wayne's behavior. During the first visit, she and Glen talked about Wayne's temper. I suggested that they bring Wayne for some individual therapy and that they attend a parenting class at the nearby community college.

At the first parenting meeting, Glen and Theresa shared their problem. The teacher told them Connie was on the right track—if Wayne wouldn't leave the room, they should separate from Wayne.

"What should I do when he pounds on my door?" asked Theresa.

"Tell him ahead of time that you'll talk to him as soon as he's calm," said the teacher.

"What if he breaks the door down?" asked Theresa.

"Let him know he'll have to earn money for a new one," said the teacher. "You can also get him a punching bag and help him practice hitting his pillow when he's calm so he's planning an outlet for his feelings ahead of time."

"What about exercise?" asked Glen. "Is that a good way to get a kid to cool down?"

"That's another way to release feelings," said the teacher. "Talk with Wayne about all these methods and see what he wants to do."

The next family council, Theresa shared the information from the parenting class.

Wayne decided he wanted to hit a pile of pillows in his room.

Connie and Wayne practiced punching the pillows—and giggling.

Wayne also wanted to see what the punching bags were like.

"I'll help you," said Glen.

They looked online and saw a blow-up punching bag filled with sand in the bottom. Wayne could knock it over, and it would stand up again. Wayne thought it was cool, so they ordered him one.

The next time Wayne had a temper tantrum, he lay on the living room floor, kicking and screaming. He refused to go to his room, so the family separated to their rooms.

After they were gone, Wayne ran to his room and punched his bed. He kicked his dirty clothes around the room and fell on his punching bag crying.

When he quieted, Theresa opened his door and sat by him, rubbing his back. "How do you feel?"

Wayne hid his face.

"I'll bet it felt good to get that anger out."

Wayne turned to her, and a faint smile flickered on his face.

Connie hugged Wayne when he came out of his room. "High five, buddy!"

Wayne looked up at her. He wasn't perfect, but he continued to improve. His temper tantrums lessened over time.

Children act out because of an unmet need.

Wayne spent several sessions with me in therapy. We talked about his father calling him "bad." Theresa, Glen, and I told him that wasn't true. He was a good kid. Theresa and Glen reminded him of specific incidents where he had helped at home and times when he had been kind to his brothers and sisters. Wayne's unmet need was love, and this new family was beginning to provide it. Wayne released the hurt he felt inside, and he began to see himself as a good kid.

Glen worked on building a relationship with Wayne. He took quiet moments to put his arm around Wayne when he was cheerful. "I'll bet you feel good about keeping yourself happy," Glen said. He also played ball with Wayne and took him to his baseball practices and games.

Wayne's temper tantrums lessened and, over time, disappeared.

Notice in the beginning that when Theresa talked about Wayne's problem, Glen kept quiet. He didn't have a strong enough bond with Wayne to begin to take part in the discipline—except to support Theresa.

The parenting classes also helped Theresa set clear, firm boundaries for Wayne and teach him to be respectful.

Wayne accepted the things Connie said because she had also had a temper. When Connie shared her feelings at family council, Glen was quiet again and let Theresa handle the situation.

Even though Wayne agreed to go to his room, he wasn't sophisticated enough to follow through at first. Since Wayne refused, the family had enough presence of mind, per Connie's suggestion, to separate themselves.

Sometimes a family needs some outside support. Therapy and parenting classes are good places to find it. There may be some extenuating circumstances where anger is concerned, so consult a professional if you have any questions. Wayne had some anger issues with his birth father, and he worked through them in therapy.

But Wayne also continued to heal in the loving family he had. His relationship with Glen grew. Connie told Wayne that she wasn't bad because she had a temper, and he wasn't either. Wayne learned to talk about his feelings and punch his bag and pillows. His anger receded.

Wayne is now an adult. He has a great relationship with Glen and considers him a father figure. The two of them enjoy their time together. Wayne is grateful for the healing power of love.

Blending a family is a slow, difficult process even when everyone is working together. Since family councils help members pull together, they are especially helpful. Talk, talk, talk, and love each other.

> ## "Love is all we have, the only way that each can help the other."
>
> —*EURIPIDES*

Here is another story of a family I worked with.

Jonathan, age 7, was often in a bad mood. When he hit his brothers,

Later that week, Barry told his mom and sisters that Dale had walked away from situations a couple of times, but he hadn't lost his cool in a week.

"There's not an immediate cure," said Mom, "but I'm glad things are better."

"I am, too," said Barry.

Note that the family supported Barry by giving him ideas for how to take care of his problem, but he left the solution to Barry. If your children are still little, teach them your family values in working with others, and guide them in keeping themselves safe.

> **"Holding on to anger is like grasping a hot coal with the intent of throwing it at someone else; you are the one who gets burned."**
>
> —*BUDDHA*

ᴄᴏ TEENS' ISSUES ᴄᴏ
VIDEO GAME ADDICTION

Today's youth are bombarded with electronics. From the time children are tiny, they have picture book apps, videos, and games that are instructive and intellectually challenging. These programs are available on phones, tablets, and computers. Even though these games and apps are enriching and stimulating, they can become addictive if teens have unlimited use of them with no adult supervision. Boundaries are important to help kids discipline themselves.

Bentley and his twin sister, Angora, age 13, loved to play video games. Mario Kart was their favorite. Mom helped them set up the game so they could race with their cousins who lived in distant cities around the United States.

Mom, a single parent working full time and going to night school, figured the game was a great way for her children to connect with family. It also gave her a break from the kids when she needed to study for a test.

Angora played the games for a little while each day and then spent her time reading or playing with friends. Bentley, however, couldn't leave the games alone. He sneaked Mom's credit card out of her purse and downloaded several new games that his buddies said were lots of fun. His grades dropped, and he became irritable.

When Mom got her credit card bill, she was livid. After her class that night, she talked with her social work professor to ask his advice.

"You have to decide what you want to teach. Why don't you make a list of the possible methods you could use and the message each would give your boy?"

"I can do that," said Mom.

"I'd also like you to share it with the class. It's a good exercise for all of us."

Mom struggled to make her lists. This is what she came up with:

Teaching Method	Message to the Child
Angry Lecture	I am at fault, and I feel worthless.
Calm Lecture	I am at fault. You are in charge.
Doling Out Consequences	I am at fault. You are in charge.
Discussion	I am of value with no consequences.
Solution-Focused Discussion	I am of value. I can solve problems. I can direct my own life.

By the time Mom talked with Bentley, she had calmed down and decided how she could best handle the situation. She used family council time to talk with both the children. The twins were so close that they would tell each other what happened anyway. She didn't want Angora to feel left out, and she thought maybe the three of them could solve the problem together.

At their meeting, Mom showed the charges for the games to both children. They'd never seen a credit card bill before and were very interested in the bill itself. She also had a printout of Bentley's grades she'd obtained from his teachers.

Bentley hung his head when he saw his grades.

Mom put a hand on his shoulder. "We have a problem here. How are we going to solve it?"

"I don't know," said Bentley.

"Let's brainstorm some solutions," said Mom.

"I'll pay for the games," said Bentley.

"Maybe you could do extra jobs," said Angora. "I'll help you."

"I should earn the money myself," said Bentley.

"That's very nice," said Mom. "But what about using a credit card at your age?"

"It's not cool," said Bentley.

"What will help you remember not to do it again?" asked Mom.

"Hide it," said Angora.

"You don't have to hide it," said Bentley. "I won't use it again."

"What about playing the games too much?" asked Mom.

"But I like to play with my cousins," said Bentley.

"Are there other ways you could spend time with them?" asked Mom.

"Mario Kart is a free game," said Bentley.

"You could video chat," said Angora.

"I could text," said Bentley.

"You could email," said Mom.

"Emails are no fun," said Bentley.

"You could draw pictures in Paint and email them," said Angora. "I like to do that."

Bentley rolled his eyes.

"Those are all great ideas," said Mom. "Any or all of them might work. Now what about homework?" Mom asked.

"Do it right after school," said Bentley.

"I like to do it after dinner," said Angora.

"What have we said before about getting our work done?" asked Mom. "What's the rule in this family?"

"Work before play." Bentley sighed.

"I guess we haven't been following it, have we?" said Mom.

Bentley looked up at her. "That's why I want to get my homework done after school so I can play the games at night after dinner."

"Good idea," said Mom.

"Then I'll do my homework right after school so we can play together," said Angora. "But maybe some days I want to play with my friends and do homework after dinner."

"Angora, you and Bentley don't have to do things just the same," said Mom.

At the family council meeting, did Mom achieve her goal of helping Bentley feel that he could solve problems and direct his own life? Did he feel of value in the discussion? He seemed to have internalized the discussion, but it would be a while until the family knew that for sure.

Bentley was definitely on his way to making changes in his life, but the real feelings of value would come as he paid back the money, left the credit card alone, and disciplined himself to play only after his homework was done.

Notice when Angora suggested Mom hide the credit card, Bentley said he wouldn't use it again. Some basic trust had already been established in this family. Bentley had enough internal control to say he wouldn't use it again.

This family didn't return for therapy after they solved this problem, so I don't know the long-term ending to their story. Mom and the children may have had to revisit this problem in the future, but for the moment they had made the necessary course correction.

Some parents worry about letting children have a say in what is to happen. If children are allowed to have input in this process, they will usually come up with something tougher than the parents would choose. We are all harder on ourselves than others are.

> ## "It is easier to build strong children than to repair broken men."
>
> —FREDERICK DOUGLASS

NEGOTIATING THE MEDIA

For generations, families have had discussions about media. Back when the American West was being settled, a pioneer father forbade his son to read *Twenty Thousand Leagues Under the Sea* by Jules Verne. Novels were a waste of time, he said. After his son went to bed, the father picked up the book out of curiosity. He stayed up all night reading the novel. He told his son at breakfast the next morning it was a good story and his son could read it.

Printed literature, radio, telephone, television, computers, internet, cell phones, email, Facebook, and Twitter—each generation has had to decide how their family will interact with the media.

When our children were young, we held a family council about the type of media we would allow into our home. Then we established rules about how much television everyone could watch. During a brainstorming session, one of the children suggested an ingenious plan that we used for years. Each person could watch one hour of TV a day and then "buy" extra time by reading.

Since we had only one television, the kids took turns choosing what to watch.

After family council each week, they sat down with the TV guide and worked out a plan where each of them chose a show they all wanted to watch. They bargained back and forth until they had a plan for the next seven days.

The TV facilitated great lessons in sharing and cooperation for our family. It also encouraged extra reading so they could watch additional programs.

The electronic age has changed a lot since our children were young, and this model won't be complete enough to handle the scope of today's media. But use these basic principles to tailor the selection of your own plan:

* Hold a family council.
* Decide the types of media you will allow in your home.
* Set time limit guidelines.
* Listen to other suggestions that might augment your program.
* Talk about negotiation skills and discuss working together.

> ## "There's no road map on how to raise a family: it's always an enormous negotiation."
>
> —MERYL STREEP

LEARNING FROM MISTAKES

Sometimes the most valuable lessons we learn in life come from our mistakes. Allowing children enough freedom to take action and make decisions on their own can be a good teaching tool as they learn to direct their own lives.

The important key for parents is to keep a good enough relationship with their children that they can talk through events to help the child define these things:

* What the child has learned
* What the child will do next time he or she is in the situation

Valeen was so excited when she turned 16. She got her driver's license and a new cell phone for her birthday. Within the first week of receiving these, she took her school friends out for tacos during their lunch hour. On the way back, she received a call from another friend. She slowed the car, pulled to the side of the road, and looked down to answer the phone. However, she didn't come to a complete stop before she took her eyes from the road, and she crashed into a utility pole, denting her fender.

Valeen was in therapy with me for another issue and came in to my office later that day, despondent. She was sure her parents would never let her drive again. We talked about what she had learned from this experience and decided how she could solve her problem.

She would call a family council and let her parents know how sorry she was. She would pay for the damage to the car with the money she earned at her part-time job, and she would promise to put her phone on vibrate and leave it in her purse while driving.

We talked about how grateful she should be that she only hit a utility pole as she was going ten miles an hour. The accident could have been a lot worse.

Valeen became a wiser person because of the accident. She learned to . . .

* Understand the consequences of her actions.
* Become more proficient in problem-solving.
* Develop better communication with her parents.
* Feel gratitude for her blessings.

We learn more from our mistakes than from our victories.

DRUG AND ALCOHOL ABUSE

Teen dependence on drugs and alcohol often indicates familial relationship problems. Many times one of the more sensitive family members can become the addict and the so-called family problem. When the family seeks help for the substance abuser, the process of healing will often lead the entire family to wellness and bring synergy to the family.

Mark, age 17, liked to drink and do drugs with his friends on the weekends. His sister, Nora, age 16, felt frantic when he left the house with the guys. She knew he shot up at the parties. He'd tried to get Nora to come with him, but she refused. She also knew he snuck some of his father's beer every night from the fridge.

Mark's brother, Todd, age 10, didn't seem to notice what was happening. Amy, age 8, clung to Nora and cried when Mark left with his friends.

Mom knew about Mark's alcohol problem, but she ignored it. He was Mom's favorite child, and everyone in the family knew it, including Dad, who sat in front of the TV after work and drank until bedtime.

One Friday night, Mark was caught with his friends in a drug bust and held by the police. Since Mom was out of town at her sister's, Dad put Mark in an adolescent treatment facility covered by the family's insurance. Dad told Mark he'd amount to nothing, and he berated and bullied Mark all the way to the center.

Nora was sick to her stomach when she found out. She sent Mark a text, but Dad had Mark's phone and read it. Dad yelled at Nora and grounded her for the next week. Todd built a space ship with his Legos. Amy cried.

When Mom returned from her sister's and heard Mark was in a facility, she and Dad alternated between yelling at each other and not speaking for two days.

Mark's therapist at the treatment center asked everyone to come in for a family meeting. Dad didn't want to go. Mom said that if he didn't attend, she'd leave him and take the children, and he'd never see them again. She was sure the therapist would blame Dad and his alcoholism as the reasons Mark also drank.

The therapist brought the family into a room in the therapy center, sat Mom and Dad together on one sofa, and sat the children on another sofa. Mom squirmed away from Dad, and Dad turned his back on Mom. Nora cuddled next to Mark and held Amy on her lap. Todd sat on the floor and took a race car out of his pocket.

The therapist invited Mark to share his feelings. Mark told the family he had set a goal to not use drugs or drink any more. Both parents began to talk over Mark—Mom was shocked that he had used drugs. The therapist invited them to be quiet and let Mark finish.

Mark went on to say that his mother put him on a pedestal and thought he was perfect. He wasn't perfect; he was just a kid trying to figure life out. His dad treated him like he was a criminal, but he wasn't. He was an OK person. He didn't like the pedestal or the prison his parents put him in. He couldn't be himself with either one.

Both a pedestal and a prison confine a person.

Dad could see that Mark had hurt Mom's feelings. He put his hand on her shoulder.

The therapist thanked Mark for sharing his feelings and for his hard work during the past week. Then she turned to Mom and Dad. The therapist thanked Mom and Dad for waiting to speak until Mark finished. She looked at everyone in the group and focused her attention on the parents. "The most important relationship in this family is yours."

Parents need to stand together.

Mom hung her head and moved a little closer to Dad.

The girls shared their feelings: Nora shared her fear, and Amy shared her sadness.

Then the therapist asked Todd how he felt about his family.

"My family can't get along, so I'm never going to have a family. I like my cars and my Legos. They don't fight."

Obviously this family had a lot of work to do.

Dad committed to attend Alcoholics Anonymous meetings—not to quit drinking, but just to see what they were like. Mom refused to go to a Codependency group, but Dad threatened to take the children and leave if she didn't. Mom went.

Mark continued to see the therapist on an outpatient basis. As he worked through his problems, he asked his family to come to his sessions once in a while for a family meeting so he could share his feelings. As time went by, the family began to hold their own councils at home. They were able to talk about issues they had never discussed before. They began to solve dilemmas better than they had in the past.

Whenever Mom and Dad fell back into their old ways of treating him, Mark reminded them of the pedestal and prison metaphor.

Mom and Dad developed a better relationship than they had before. Mark's problem forced them to work together. Notice the tight bond several of the children had with each other. Children are very wise. Many times we don't appreciate their insight and understanding.

The family slowly learned to communicate and allow everyone to have feelings. Healing was a day-to-day process, and working in the family council setting became a catalyst for much of the closeness this family developed.

This scenario played over and over in my office—parents trying to figure out how to be parents, and kids trying to figure out how to be kids. Family councils are not the answer to cure all family ills, but they can be a stimulant for communication and understanding while we all try to figure out our relationships.

If you have teens with a drug or alcohol problem, seek professional help. Check your community resources. Here are two hotline resources.

http://www.recovery-world.com/National-Hotline-Phone-Numbers.html

http://www.niaaa.nih.gov/alcohol-health/support-treatment

☙ CREATING FAMILY UNITY ❧
WORKING TOGETHER AS A FAMILY

There are lots of lessons to be learned from family councils, but one of the most important ones is how to help the family work together as a cohesive unit. If the family has collaborated over time during the day-to-day activities, they will be able to pull together through a crisis.

During one cold winter week, Dad was out of town on a business trip. He usually took the garbage out before work, but he was gone, and it had piled up in the kitchen. Snow and then freezing rain covered the ground outside. In the kitchen, Mom looked at the trash. She couldn't stand it any longer, so she slipped on her flip-flops, picked up the can, and skated carefully to the outside dumpster. After depositing the garbage, she made her way back to the door. Just as she reached the back steps, she slipped and fell on her left ankle. She heard a crunch and pain seared up her leg and down into her foot, taking her breath away. She knew it was either badly sprained or broken.

She hobbled into the house, grabbed an ice pack, and called a neighbor to drive her to the emergency room. Four hours later, she came home with crutches and a boot for her fractured ankle.

The neighbor settled Mom on the couch and said she'd check on her in a couple of hours. When the kids came home from school, they found Mom asleep on the sofa.

"What do we do?" asked Rose, age 17.

"Let her sleep," said Richard, age 14.

"I'm getting a snack," said Fuller, age 13.

Mary, age 8, cried quietly.

Rose herded everyone into the kitchen. "Let's have our own emergency family council. Mom's not going to be able to do much for a while."

Fuller stuffed a piece of leftover pizza in his mouth. "I'm not doing any extra work."

"I will," said Mary. "I want to help so Mom will get better."

"How about those who want to help can?" said Richard. "Let's put another bean in our party jar when we do an extra job."

"No fair," said Fuller.

Rose turned to Fuller. "Remember, when we get 100 beans, we voted to go to the indoor water park with the slides and the wave machine—*your* favorite place."

"Oh, man!" Fuller gulped a glass of milk and stuffed more pizza into his mouth. "I guess I'll help."

"Great," said Rose. "We're all in."

"What should we do?" asked Richard.

"Everybody get your own snack and clean up," said Rose. "Then dinner. Let's have spaghetti. I'll cook the meat and sauce. Who wants to cook the noodles?"

"Me," said Fuller. "I'll make them mushy like I like them."

"We know." Richard rolled his eyes. "I'll grate the cheese and get a loaf of French bread from the freezer."

"I want warm bread," said Rose.

"I'll heat it in the oven," said Richard.

"What about me?" asked Mary.

"You can warm up two cans of green beans," said Rose. "That's a great dinner. Meeting adjourned."

"Wait," said Mary, "we didn't give compliments or vote."

"Nothing to vote on, silly." Fuller flipped Mary's braid.

"Stop!" hissed Rose.

"Shhh," said Mary.

"Is that you, kids?" asked Mom.

Mom had to wear the boot for six weeks. Things didn't always go as smoothly as organizing dinner that first night had, but everyone pitched in to help. Since this family had held council meetings for years, the kids were used to working together. They did laundry and extra cleaning so the household ran as normally as possible.

At the end of the first three weeks, the kids had done enough jobs and added enough beans to their party jar to earn a trip to the water park. By then Mom was up and about and could go with them and watch.

This family has given their children a great gift—the ability to organize and serve. The parents, in this instance, were both giving, loving people. The children picked up on their example. There are times when children learn lessons just by watching the adults they live with. Even though Dad was out of town, these children knew he helped Mom out by taking out the garbage, and they did the same.

After this incident, Mom was heard to say, "Winter rule—wear non-skid shoes to take out the garbage."

WORKING TOGETHER
IN THE NEIGHBORHOOD

When our children were growing up, there were crises with more than just our family involved. Our eight-year-old boy, Chris, had a best friend, Roger, who lived next door. The boys were fascinated with fire. They loved to take their magnifying glasses and focus the sun's rays onto a leaf or some berries and burn them.

Roger's little brother Jim, age 6, wanted to make fire like Chris and Roger. He didn't have a magnifying glass, so he got some matches from the kitchen and started a palm tree on fire in his yard. The dry base of the tree caught quickly and leapt to the green at the top of the tree. When I heard the crackling and saw what was happening, I called the fire department (Roger and Jim's parents were deaf).

I raced for the garden hose, but it was only a small trickle and couldn't begin to squelch the leaping flames. Soon the fire truck arrived. We stood, watching and shivering with fear. Shortly the blaze was out. Jim was scared, and so were the older boys.

Chris put his arms around me and buried his face in my arms. I hugged him and said, "I'll bet you were scared. We were all afraid. We could have lost everything."

"I know," he said.

I asked him, "What will help you remember not to play with fire again?"

"It wasn't my fault." He looked up at me. "It was Jim's fault."

I ignored his defense and asked again what would help him remember to not play with fire again.

"I don't know," he said.

I suggested it might be a good idea to have the fire chief come talk to our family, and Roger and Jim were welcome to listen also.

The neighbors were supportive of the idea, and the fire chief visited with the boys the next day. The chief was kind, but he was explicit about the dangers of fire. He showed the boys pictures of what could have happened if the blaze had gotten out of hand. He also gave us an address of a recent fire where a house burned down, and we took the boys to see the charred rubble.

Chris decided on his own that he didn't want to play with his magnifying glass any more. He was sorry for what had happened.

We talked with the neighbors, and Roger put his magnifying glass away also.

We didn't hold a formal family council with the neighbors, but we did work together to help the boys see the consequences of what could have happened if we hadn't caught the fire quickly.

I am grateful I heard the fire; otherwise, our dear neighbors would have lost their house. All three boys learned a lesson. We never know when our actions might benefit those around us.

> # "It takes a village to raise a child."
>
> ## —*African Proverb*

Chapter 3:

Parental Roles in Family Councils

❦ Interaction with ❧ Your Children

Listen

The childhood years are skill-building years. It's important for children to develop talents and explore their interests. Sometimes we as parents try to plug our children into the avenues we think best, when in reality, our children are the ones who need to make their own choices. It's also a good learning experience for them to try things and realize, on their own, that they love an activity or that they don't really like it.

Mike, age 10 and the youngest of four, loved to draw. He knew everyone in the family played the piano, but he didn't want to take piano lessons. He wanted to enroll in an art class. He complained to his older brother Joe, age 17, that Mom wouldn't listen to him. Joe suggested Mike put his name on the agenda for the next family council. Joe explained that if Mike brought up the art lessons at family council, maybe Mom would take note since it was an official family council.

Mike put his name on the agenda and explained his problem at the next family council. At first, Mom didn't want to hear what Mike had to say. She said he could take the art lessons, but he had to have piano lessons also.

Mike sighed. "I don't want to play the piano. I just want to learn to draw." He said if he had to do some kind of music, he would like to join the school band's percussion section and learn to play the bells. After all, they were kind of like the piano.

Dad suggested that Mike have a chance to try the bells and the art lessons. Mike promised that if he didn't practice his drawing and his bells, he would take the piano lessons. Mom agreed to give him a chance.

"Thanks for listening," said Joe.

Mom looked at her hands and then glanced up at Mike. "You've tried to tell me this before, and I haven't really heard you. I'm sorry for that. I'll try to listen more often."

Joe said he liked being in this family because they had all learned something from this incident. Everyone does have different talents and abilities and should be able to try the things they want to learn about.

> "The beginning of this love is the will to let those we love be perfectly themselves, the resolution not to twist them to fit our own image."
>
> —THOMAS MERTON

Establish a Routine

It's important to establish a routine in your home. Children thrive on knowing what will come next. It gives them a sense of security.

Jason, age three, stayed home with his grandmother while his mother was in the hospital having his baby sister. His grandmother made oatmeal for breakfast. Jason didn't want the oatmeal. His mother always toasted him a frozen waffle with strawberry jam.

Grandma lived a long way away and didn't visit very often, so she didn't know the routine. Jason insisted he wanted a waffle.

Grandmother knelt down beside him so she could look him in the eyes, and said, "Jason, why don't you tell me the things you do in your day with Mom? I know it's hard to have her gone."

Jason smiled and hugged her. He then outlined their morning routine. They ate toasted waffles with strawberry jam, and Jason rode his trike down the street to the park. They were swinging when Mom and Dad called with the news that the baby was born. Both Mom and baby were fine.

On the way home from the park, Jason asked if they could read his favorite books before lunch.

This family is a little too young to begin a formal family council, but look at the skills that are already being developed with Jason.

* He feels valued because grandmother knelt down, looked him in the eyes, and listened to him.
* A definite family routine is in place so Jason knows what to expect and can outline it for others.
* He and grandmother are cooperating with each other
* They have had fun together.
* They spent special time together.

Routine brings security.

STAY POSITIVE

When children are irritated or angry, it's hard for you to remain positive. It takes practice and self-discipline to separate yourself emotionally from your attacker and stay out of the fray.

Billy, age 8, sat cross-legged in the middle of the floor, rocking. He had arrived two days ago from his mother's home and was spending the summer with his dad's family. (His parents never married—Billy was the result of an affair.)

The family was gathered for their weekly meeting. "We'd love to have you join our family council," said Dad. "We meet together every week to discuss our plans and have fun together."

"I don't want to be here," said Billy. "I want to be home with my friends."

"We're glad to have you with us for the summer," said Billy's stepmother "We'd love to be friends with you as well."

Billy looked at the floor. "No."

Dad turned back to the family council. "Compliments all around. I'll begin."

Billy open and shut his fists. "No compliments for me."

Dad continued. "Mom, thanks for that good meal last night. I do love your pot roast." He turned to Nora, age 12. "I appreciate your cleaning off the patio on Saturday. It looks so much better. You really worked hard."

Billy slammed one fist into his other hand. "Patio. I made tire tracks with my bike. Messed up your job."

Dad remained calm and turned to Tom, age 14. "Moving Mrs. Jones on Saturday was a lot of hard work. Thanks for lending your strong back to the cause. You saved my bacon."

Billy rocked again. "Bacon. I want bacon for dinner."

"Billy, thanks for being with us during our meeting," said Dad.

Billy jumped up. "I told you I don't want to be here. I'm going to tell my mother that you're beating me."

"Oh, come off it," said Tom. "You're putting all of us in a bad mood."

"Tom's right," said Dad. "We'd love to have you stay at our meeting, but if you'd rather not, you can find something to do in your room."

"There'll be Mom's special brownies and games after we finish," said Nora.

"I don't care." Billy looked around. "I'm going to my room."

"You're welcome to join us when you're ready," said Dad.

"In your dreams." Billy stomped off.

The family continued their meeting and, afterward, got out UNO Attack. Mom cut the brownies and dished up some ice cream. The smell of chocolate floated through the house.

The game began with the whirr of the machine and cards flying here and there. Laughter accompanied each gush of cards.

Billy poked his head around the corner of the hall and drummed his fingers on the wall.

"Hey, Billy." Dad turned to look at him. "Join us."

Billy leaped back. "I don't play *cards*."

"Suit yourself," Dad said.

The family continued to eat and play. Billy watched.

"I want more brownies." Tom got up from the table. He looked at Billy. "I'll cut you one."

"OK." Billy stepped forward, took it on a napkin, and retreated into the shadow of the hallway.

After the family finished, they each went their own way. Billy sat at the table, pushed the UNO Attack button, and watched the cards fly. He smiled.

"Play with us next time," said Nora as she walked by.

"Maybe," said Billy. "Maybe."

Note the fact that Dad tried to include Billy at the beginning of the council, but Billy only wanted to disturb the family. It was not OK for Billy to upset the entire family routine.

If Dad had begged Billy to stay and tried to do just what Billy wanted, it would have given Billy too much power in the family. If Dad had forced Billy to stay, it would have caused Billy to get angrier than he already was.

It took some self-discipline on Dad's part, but he respected Billy enough to let him have his own feelings and find his own way in this situation. He gave Billy permission to separate himself from the group. Notice that it wasn't a negative, punishing separation. As the family played the game, Dad really wanted Billy to join them. But when Billy rejected him, Dad backed off.

This family had clearly taught the importance of positive consequences before because the entire family helped Billy, even the children.

* Dad told Billy he could spend time in the bedroom.
* Tom gave Billy a brownie.
* Nora invited him to play UNO Attack next time.

Billy had lots of feelings inside about who he is and what life held for him. There was a lot of love in this family—enough to help Billy heal if he would be willing to accept it. As I worked with youth like this in a counseling setting, many of them came to be at peace with themselves if they were willing to be proactive in their healing process.

> ## "Nothing will work unless you do."
>
> —*MAYA ANGELOU*

BE WHAT YOU WANT TO TEACH

Children follow example. Have you ever watched a two-year-old pick up a newspaper and sit in a chair to read it just like her father?

MODEL FOR YOUR CHILDREN.

If you want your children to eat healthy foods, then your family must eat healthy foods. In our family, several of our children came born with more sophisticated tastes than others. Some loved spices, onions, and garlic from a young age. Others enjoyed vegetables right from the beginning. The rest learned to like them as they grew older.

There are many things your children can learn from your example. If you are kind and loving to those around you, your children will pick up your pattern. For example, we are a hugging family, so our children and grandchildren have picked up the pattern. Everybody hugs in our family.

When you meet in a family council each week to discuss your problems, plan your activities, set your goals—even set your menus or manage your money, and your children will become aware of the way you do things.

TELL YOUR CHILD
WHAT YOU WANT HIM OR HER TO DO.

Give your child clear directions for the behavior you are looking for. For example, say, "Put ten percent in your savings account, and the rest is yours to spend."

When I was a young mother, I sat in church, waiting for the meeting to start, and I watched a mother see her young son hit his baby sister. She snatched his hand away and slapped it several times, saying, "Don't hit."

We must be careful what we teach. Sometimes our actions speak louder than our words.

Model behavior for your children and talk about it at family council to aid the development of healthy behaviors.

Help your child

become the best he or she can be.

Children come with their own personalities, and our task as parents is to help them learn the principles we feel are important for them to become strong, functional adults.

I think it's good for children to understand that they are unique. They have their own strengths and weaknesses. Let them define themselves and set their own goals.

Family councils are not a solution to all our problems, but they are a vehicle for defining a family. As we meet, plan, and discuss, we let our children know who we are and what we stand for.

Give your child the gift of a great heritage.

Include Everyone in the Finances

Schools of thought vary as to whether to include the children in family finance information or not. Sometimes sharing with older children is helpful because their wants and needs can become very expensive.

Assess your finances and your situation, and talk with your children as you think it wise. Here is an instance where sharing with children was helpful.

A client of mine, Sage, thought her parents were too tight with money when she was a teenager. But as she grew older and learned to manage her own finances, she could see that her parents weren't miserly. They just didn't have much money.

Sage, age 16, wanted a new computer for her birthday.

"All my friends have one," she said. "Other parents are more generous than you. You're stingy with your money."

Dad took a deep breath and let Sage's biting words go before he put his name on the agenda for family council.

At the next meeting he shared his problem. "As you know, the company downsized this past year, and I had to take a pay cut. I've been looking for another job in the area, but nothing's come open yet."

"We thought we'd include you in the finances," said Mom to Sage. "I made a chart. On the left is the income—Dad's paycheck and the money I earn from tutoring. On the right there is a list of our expenses."

"We wanted to get you involved," said Dad. "I would love to buy you a new computer, Sage. Let's take a look at the budget and see if we can find any extra money."

For the next half hour, the family looked over the figures to see if there was anywhere to carve out a little money for a computer. They found an extra hundred dollars in gas money if everyone coordinated their errands. In several months there would be enough for a computer—especially if Sage took her lunch every day, rather than buying. She could also save her clothing allowance.

Sage learned several lessons from this experience.

* Sage saw the workings of a monthly budget firsthand.
* She felt more grown-up because her parents trusted her enough to include her in the solution to the problem.
* Her problem-solving skills increased.
* She learned to be solution-focused with her money.
* She felt closer to her parents because they confided in her.

Sage got her computer in a few months. She appreciated it more than she would have if she hadn't gone through this process. She felt her quality of life had improved because she had learned to manage money.

Talk together to decide if this would be a good idea in your own family. Children are often much more willing to save their money if they know the entire financial story and if they have a goal in mind.

Decide what your family financial rules will be. Discuss them at family council. We decided that when the children turned twelve, they had to pay half for items such as clothing, nail polish, hair accessories, and electronic games. Some families ask their teens to work part-time to pay for their gas and car insurance if they have a vehicle.

Take some time as a family to decide what will be best for you. Family council is a great place to work this through.

> "You are balancing your money for life, and a critical part of balance is having some money to enjoy."
>
> —ELIZABETH WARREN

SEEING THE GOOD IN YOUR CHILDREN

There are times when our teens have greater insight to life than adults do. Sometimes, as parents, we don't appreciate the goodness in our children because we want them to fit into our mold. I love watching families where children are allowed to march to the beat of a different drum. It expands the scope of the entire family, allowing everyone to grow.

A father once sat in my office with his head in his hands. "This is not how my life was supposed to end up—with court-ordered counseling and parenting classes. I'm a major in the Air Force. I can command my

F-16 to fly faster than the speed of sound, but I can't control my own kids."

"Two of the words you just used don't work for people, especially teens: *command* and *control*." I leaned forward in my chair. "People don't work like machines."

"I know that—at least I thought I knew it." Dad sighed.

'This week your assignment is to hold a family council, like your parenting class suggested. Just listen to your children. Get to know them."

"I'm used to standing at the podium, talking the new pilots through the training strategy."

I sat forward. "Don't stand to conduct this meeting. Don't even sit at a table. Gather in the living room on the comfortable couches in a circle so everyone is on equal footing."

Dad didn't want to hold a meeting with his children, but he promised. And he did need to get the court off his back. How could that blankety-blank neighbor have turned him in for yelling and taking a belt to his boy? He was in his own backyard for pity's sake, and he wasn't actually going to beat Len—just scare him into shaving his head. Nothing had gone right since his wife, Phyllis, had died.

Dad banged the back door as he entered the house and looked at his three kids sitting at the table doing their homework. "We need to have a meeting."

Len, age 14, raised his head. "What about?"

Dad clenched his teeth. "It's my assignment. OK?" His voice sounded harsh.

"We don't want to talk if you're going to be angry," said Suzie, age 18.

"I have a paper due tomorrow," said Ernie, age 16. "I'm too busy."

"You'll just lecture us," said Suzie. "We don't want that."

"I'm only supposed to listen," said Dad. "That's all."

Ernie turned toward Dad. "I have about half an hour."

"Fine," said Dad. "Let's sit in the living room where we can be comfortable."

Everyone sat.

Dad leaned forward on the couch with his elbows on his knees. "Look, I know things haven't been good since Mom died. She was the peacemaker, the one you talked to, not me."

"You're right," said Suzie. "We talk to each other now, but not to you."

"I have to change that," said Dad. "Correction, I *want* to change that."

"You're never going to accept my religious beliefs," said Ernie. "My life doesn't concern you—in fact, you said I'm a lily-livered coward that has to rely on—"

"I know, I know." Dad cut him off. "Don't repeat it."

"Why not? It's burned into my brain forever."

"I can't say I won't do it again," said Dad. "But I'm going to try. If religion is your thing . . ."

"The point is," said Ernie, "I'm not a bad kid. I have straight A's, I'm on the debate team, I don't do drugs or alcohol, and I go to church. That should be good—no, *outstanding*—in any parent's book."

"I know, I know." Dad shook his head. "I said I'll try." He looked at Len. "Religion is one thing, but purple and orange hair is another."

"I like my hair." Len ran the palm of his hand across the purple spike on the crown of his head. Then he stroked his fingers through the orange curls near his neck.

"The leader of the parenting group told me I should pick my battles, and hair wasn't one of them." Dad rubbed his own crew cut. "But I'm used to the military. How can you stand to look like that?"

"Dad," said Suzie. "Quit while you're ahead."

"Trouble is," said Len, "he's not ahead where I'm concerned—ever."

Dad focused his gaze on Len. Tears watered his eyes. "You're the most like your mother of all you kids. You have a lot of talent."

One tear, and then two, fell onto Len's cheeks. "I can't draw near as good as her right now, but I'm going to practice until I'm as good as she is—was."

Dad stared at his hands. "I *want* you to do that. I'll honor the commitment Mom made to you. Keep your grades up, and I'll pay for the best art school in the country."

Len smiled. "I'm more organized than a lot of the kids in my art class. They put things off till the last minute, and I get things done when I'm supposed to."

"I know," said Dad. "But there are times when I'd just like to throw you down and shave you bald."

"Dad," said Suzie.

Dad held up his hands. "But I'm not going to do that." He turned to Suzie. "You have to get on with your life. You just can't stay home and take care of us like you've taken Mom's place."

Suzie stood, facing her dad. "I love my brothers more than anything, and I'm going to be here to protect them until they're out of the house."

He put his head in his hands. "I'll try to ease up. I don't want you to give up your life because you feel like you have to protect them."

"Four years—until Len is eighteen—and my life can begin." Suzie put her hands on her hips. "I'm not leaving them alone with you."

Dad glanced up at her and then down at the floor. "Look, I'll back off. I promise."

"I don't know that right now," said Suzie, "but I appreciate the offer. We'll just have to wait and see."

"At least register for a couple of courses at the community college," said Dad. "Go to class while the boys are in school."

"I guess I could," said Suzie. "But I'm scared. What if I can't do it? You've told me yourself that I don't measure up."

Dad rose from his seat and gave her an awkward hug. "I'm not good at this, but I'll try. You do measure up. You'll make a wonderful wife and mother."

Suzie jerked back from him. "I will do that *after* I get a degree in creative writing." She put her hands on her hips. "You don't know me at all."

Dad put his hands up again. "Okay, okay. All I can say is that I'll try."

Ernie pulled his phone out of his pocket. "I have to go, Dad. Is that all you wanted?"

Dad dropped his head. "Yes."

Len stood. "Let's do this again. I liked it."

"Me, too," said Ernie. "Me, too."

Family council meetings for this family have a long way to go, but this was a good beginning. Dad and the kids started to talk to each other. The children came in for several sessions with their father, and tension in the family eased somewhat. Through family council meetings, they organized themselves so that the bulk of the work didn't fall to Suzie. She did get into a university, finished her degree, and married (in that order). Ernie went off to a divinity school to become a minister, and Len enrolled in art school.

Family councils became a mediating force for good in this family. They enhanced communication and gave Dad a better understanding of relationships. Dad is still a military man, but he has open interaction with the kids, and he loves having his children and grandchildren around.

> ## "Be yourself; everyone else is already taken."
>
> —OSCAR WILDE

◯ PARENTS' ISSUES ◯

BECOMING A SINGLE PARENT—DIVORCE

Trials come into all of our lives, and one of the greatest upheavals a family may face is that of divorce.

In the bloom of youth, we fall in love. As maturity makes its way into our lives, there are times when adjustments are needed in relationships.

A childless couple can let their affiliation go and decide to put their energies into new associations—with no one but the couple hurt in the process. But if there are children in the family, parents have a special responsibility to do everything in their power to save their marriage.

Here are two truisms I discovered over the years:

If two people are willing to work on their relationship, it can most likely be saved.

If only one person is prepared to change in a relationship, it may not survive.

Sophia and her husband, Mason, had been married for about eight years. Two young children blessed their lives: Alexander, age 2, and Addison, age . Sophia knew Mason had changed over the past couple of years. He seemed detached and was gone from the house for long stretches of time. He had always wanted things his way, but now he was openly critical of her and the children.

One day, he came home to tell her he had a boyfriend and wanted to live an alternative lifestyle. Sophia felt devastated. She told her husband she wanted to save their marriage, but he wasn't interested. He had another significant relationship. He moved out. She didn't want a divorce, but she needed one now. Her dream of a happy married life shattered at that moment.

She found a therapist to help her deal with the grief and anger that felt all-consuming. Her marriage was gone, and there was nothing she could do about it. She and her two precious children were the whole family now.

The therapist helped her see that she needed to find peace in her own soul so she and the children could pull together as a functioning unit. They talked about family councils in one of her sessions, and Sophia decided it would be a good idea to try holding them.

She began family councils in an informal way since her children were so small. Every night they read several picture books together and finished with a Bible story. They planned their week and talked about how sad they felt because Daddy was gone.

The children became the most important thing in Sophia's life. As they grew a little older, she took some classes to keep her lab certification up. When the children were in school, she went back to work in a nearby hospital.

Family council time became very important to all of them because in family councils they had schedules to coordinate, practices to attend, homework to plan—and reading. Everyone in the family loved to finish the day together with a book, an informal family council. The children are teens now and have developed different tastes in literature, but sometimes they still read together. Family council for this little group of people facilitated emotional closeness, good communication, organization, and also a love of literature.

RAISING CHILDREN
ALONE—LOSING A SPOUSE

One of the saddest issues I worked with as a counselor was that of a young growing family grieving the loss of one of the parents. It's devastating for everyone. The grieving partner has to continue to keep the family functional and lament the loss the love of his or her life. Children will usually take their emotional clues from the parent that remains, so this is an added burden for the surviving spouse.

Sergio trudged into the house, hardly able to breathe. How could he break the news to his children that Anna, their mother and the love of his life, was dead? He opened the back door. The children left the book their grandmother was reading to them and rushed into his arms. He knelt, held them, and sobbed. He didn't have to use words—everyone knew.

The next few weeks blurred for him. His mother stayed to help with the children: Ava, age 13, and Jayden, age 8. She worried about Sergio. He seemed detached from and unresponsive to the children. He went to work every day, but he seemed to be in a world all his own.

"You have to come back to earth," his mother chided. "You have a family to raise."

"I'm too sad," said Sergio.

"Anna is not coming back, and I know she wants you to be there for the children." His mother took Sergio's hands in hers. "Let's talk with Ava and Jayden and see how they feel. They're sad."

"I can't do that," said Sergio. "I'll just cry."

"You can do it. Take some deep breaths before you start. The children need to talk."

"I'll try, but I may need you to pull me out of the hole."

"I'm already pulling you out of the hole." His mother smiled and hugged him.

Sergio chuckled. He hadn't laughed in weeks and it felt good. "All right. I'll call a family meeting, and we'll talk."

The next day Sergio called the meeting to order. "Today we need to plan. Our lives will never be the same again." Sergio broke down sobbing.

His mother came to his side and rubbed his shoulders. "Take a deep breath."

Sergio did and composed himself. "We all need to talk about how much we miss Mom."

The children shared their feelings about Mom, and the family cried together.

"I'm afraid," said Jayden.

"What about?" asked Sergio.

"What if you leave, too? Then we'll have no one."

Sergio felt his back slump into his chair as if someone had punched him. Tears filled his eyes. "I won't leave you." He looked at both the children. "I'll be here for you."

Sergio's mother smiled and hugged the children. "You're stuck with both of us." She laughed, and the children did, too. She pulled an extra chair into the family circle and placed Anna's picture on the chair. "Let's remember the good times with your mom."

Sergio wept.

Each family member told a favorite memory with Anna.

"Let's do this every week at our meeting," said Ava. "I love talking about Mom."

"Me, too," said Jayden.

The family meeting facilitated the mourning process that loomed before this family. With the help of a wise grandmother, the remaining members of this family could grieve and remember their lovely wife and mother.

Notice also Jayden's fear. Some children worry that if one parent has left them, maybe the other would also. Because of the openness and safety of this meeting, Jayden could share his worry.

One day, Sergio asked me when he would get over Anna's death. I don't think one ever gets completely "over" the death of a loved one. Anna had been the love of his life for a long time, and she will continue to be so as long as he lives.

Sergio and his family continued to include an empty chair in their council meetings. They wanted Anna with them, and this was a way to keep her close. When one of them put a tough question on the agenda that needed to be discussed, they could always ask, "What would mother say?" She was still involved her in their lives even though she was not with them anymore.

> ## "To love is so startling it leaves little time for anything else."
>
> —*EMILY DICKINSON*

STANDING TOGETHER AS PARENTS

The marital relationship should be the most viable in the family. However, in many families, there is a stronger bond between parents and children than between husband and wife. When this happens, the children don't have consistent boundaries. They learn rather quickly which parent is on their side and will give them what they want.

Here is how one family faced this problem.

Leon, age 15, glanced at his mother. "Tobias gets away with murder in this house."

"How do you figure that?" asked Mom.

Leon shrugged. "He doesn't even have to fold his laundry."

"I guarantee you were not folding laundry when you were four," said Mom.

"That was because I was your first child, and you hadn't figured out how to run a family yet," said Leon. "You're much smarter now, and Tobias should have to fold his clothes."

Tobias ran his train engine through the pile of clean laundry. "This is a tunnel through the mountain." His elbow knocked over Leon's stack of folded T-shirts.

Leon sighed in disgust. "Stop, Tobias." He turned to Mom. "See what I mean?"

Dad walked into the room. "How's the laundry brigade?"

"Great," said Mom.

"Tobias should have to fold," said Leon.

"My baby is *not* folding laundry," said Mom.

"He's old enough to fold," said Dad.

"I am not," said Tobias, running his train over to Mom's feet and hugging her leg.

"You should fold," said Dad.

"No," said Tobias, "I'm too little."

Mom frowned at Dad and took Tobias by the hand. "Let's go set up your train set in the bedroom."

In this family the parental tie between Dad and Leon was strong, and the link between Mom and Tobias was even stronger. What are the messages this couple was giving to the children? Leon may have felt put-upon or slighted. Tobias knew he was special to his mother and that he could get out of work. He would grow up not knowing his capability or his strength.

Mom wanted Tobias to have every opportunity possible during his growing-up years, so she enrolled him in a preschool at the local university. The program required the parents to attend several parenting classes.

As Mom and Dad sat in one of the meetings, they both realized they needed to stand together as far as the children were concerned.

They learned that the following happens if parents don't stand together:

* Children have inconsistent boundaries.
* They figure out how to manipulate to get their way.
* They are able to pit one parent against the other.
* They can consistently avoid work.

Mom and Dad also learned about family councils and decided to begin holding them. At the first family meeting, Dad conducted, and Mom put her name on the agenda. After compliments all around, Dad called on Mom.

Mom looked at the boys. "Dad and I have learned a few things in our parenting classes that we'd like to try."

"What?" asked Tobias.

"First," said Mom, "we all need to work in this family."

"What work?" asked Tobias.

"You and I are going to make up a job chart for the week."

"No," said Tobias. "I can't do it."

Dad got up, walked to the sofa, sat down next to Mom and put his arm around her. "Listen to Mom."

"No," said Tobias again. "I can't do it." He ran to the sofa and tried to separate Mom and Dad and sit between them.

Dad pulled Tobias onto his lap and gave him a hug. Tobias struggled away and cuddled onto Mom's lap.

"I'll help you do your work," said Mom.

"But I have to run my trains," said Tobias.

"Your trains can help us," said Mom.

Leon sighed and smiled. "It's about time."

Tobias's behavior got worse before it got better. He didn't want to help with household chores. Sometimes he refused. For instance, he wouldn't clear his dinner dishes from the table, so Mom and Dad served chocolate cake to everyone but Tobias. He hurried to clear his dishes, and Mom cut him a piece of cake.

Tobias had had life pretty easy before, and he didn't want it to change. The family set up a token economy. Tobias put a sticker on his success chart every time he completed a task so he could earn a trip to the train museum. It took about six weeks for Tobias to accept the fact that work was something he needed to do.

His teachers at preschool noticed a difference in Tobias. They reported that he had more confidence and was eager to help with new projects. His self-assurance improved as he completed his chores.

Because Mom and Dad stood together, Tobias's behavior changed. He couldn't manipulate Mom any more. He learned to be a contributing member of the family.

"Our household seems to run more smoothly," said Dad one night when he and Mom were getting ready for bed.

"I feel like I have my partner back," said Mom. "Somehow we got off course when the children came along."

Dad hugged her. "Have you noticed how Leon watches us?"

"Yes." Mom smiled. "Remember what the parenting teacher said? If you and I have the strongest relationship in our family, our children will pick up the pattern and create the same kind of connection in their marriages."

Mom has just identified one of the best gifts we as parents can give our children. If we have a loving relationship, our children will be more likely have one also. Give your children the gift of seeing a happy marriage. It's a legacy that will last a lifetime and beyond.

> ## "The only place success comes before work is in the dictionary."
>
> —*VINCE LOMBARDI*

AVOIDING CODEPENDENCE

Codependency happens when one person has an unhealthy reliance on another. Sometimes we can unwittingly love our children so much that we don't allow them to grow up. We keep them dependent on us so they never really launch themselves into adulthood. It doesn't just happen with children—it occurs in adult relationships as well.

Here are a few characteristics of codependent people:

* They see themselves as unselfish.
* They look for the negative qualities of others.
* They have a hard time making decisions.
* They believe others are incapable of taking care of themselves.

Here is how one woman overcame codependency.

Grandma complained to her friend Beata over lunch that she didn't know why her life had turned out like it had. She had devoted herself to her children, doing everything she could to make their lives easy. But her daughter Mabel, age 40, and her son Jack, age 42, were both living at home and dependent on her.

Grandma had supported Mabel for the last two years after Mabel's divorce. Mabel needed to get a job, but she just sat at home, watching soap operas all day long. Grandma felt trapped. She didn't know how to get Mabel out of the house—and if Mabel did get a job, could she keep it? Grandma was tired of spending her retirement check on her daughter. She thought she wanted to travel, but she didn't know for sure.

Beata sympathized with Grandma and suggested the two of them sell their houses and move into condos. Then they could go on cruises together and live in a warm climate during the winter months.

Grandma sighed and went on to complain that she couldn't kick out Jack and his son Abe, age 7. That was no way to treat a child. Abe had needed lots of support since his mom died of cancer last year.

"I can see some of the same codependency issues in you that I had in the early days of my marriage when my husband drank too much," said Beata. "I didn't allow him to be responsible for himself. I took too good care of him."

"What happened?" asked Grandma.

"One of my friends suggested I attend a codependency group, and those meetings saved my life and my marriage."

"What exactly is a codependent?" asked Grandma.

"It's when you do something for someone they can do for themselves."

"Oh," said Grandma. "I'm in trouble on this one."

They finished lunch, and Grandma began to think about what Beata had said.

She looked in the phone book that afternoon and found a group she could attend—they were called CoDA meetings. At the meeting she learned that other people struggled with relationships—keeping family members dependent by doing too much for them—just as she did.

That night, Grandma stood in her kitchen doorway after washing up the dinner dishes. Jack sat at the table with Abe, helping him finish his homework. Abe had a book report due the next day that he'd forgotten about. The book was too long for Abe to read in one night, so Jack said he'd read it for Abe and tell him what to write in the report. Abe sat playing a game on his phone while Jack read the book. Mabel watched *Jeopardy* on the TV.

Shockwaves of memory ran through Grandma. She'd done homework for Jack when he was a boy. She could see herself sitting at the table just like Jack. Jack was doing something for Abe that he could do for himself.

What had she done to her children? What was Jack doing to Abe?

Thoughts and questions raced through her head, and she couldn't wait for her CoDA meeting the next week.

At the meeting, she explained her situation to the members of the group and asked their advice. They suggested that she decide what to do for herself. If they told her everything, she would become codependent on them.

Everyone laughed.

"I can see that I've tried to get others to make my decisions for me," said Grandma.

"That never works," said one of the group members.

They advised Grandma that after she decided her course of action, she would need to let her family know.

One of the young mothers said that she and her family held family councils each week. "It's really helped my relationship with my children. They're learning to make their own decisions."

Grandma decided to try it—maybe it was her first step to unravel her dilemma.

At the first family council, Grandma asked everyone to give compliments to the group. She had the hardest time thinking of good things to say—especially with Mabel. Abe could think of positives about everyone. In fact, he wanted to go around the circle twice.

Grandma informed Mabel she was turning off the cable service. Mabel would have to get a job to pay for it if she wanted it turned back on. Mabel got angry and yelled at her mother, but she put in an application the following day at a temp agency.

At the next family council, Grandma reminded Jack of how she had done his homework when he was a boy. As they talked, Jack could see he wasn't doing Abe any favors by rescuing him. Abe needed to be responsible for his schoolwork.

Grandma continued to attend CoDA meetings and hold family councils. Slowly but surely, this multi-generational family began to set healthier boundaries. Everyone felt better about themselves. The situation wasn't perfect, but it was livable.

Grandma didn't sell the house and move south for the winter, but she and Mabel did take a cruise. They had so much fun that they decided to travel every winter.

Family council isn't a cure-all for codependency, but it does do the following:

* Facilitate the decision-making process
* Teach everyone to look for the good in others
* Call family members to accountability for their actions
* Help members be proactive

All these skills guard against codependency, and they foster healthy independence.

> "The lesson I was learning involved the idea that I could feel compassion for people without acting on it."
>
> —*MELODY BEATTIE*

GIVING CHILDREN TOO MUCH POWER

Sometimes children can be given so much power that it overrides common sense.

Joe, age 2, had a sore throat and hacking cough. He woke up at about midnight coughing and crying. He couldn't breathe. Dad held him and rocked him for about an hour and then gave Joe to Mom to cuddle while Dad ran to the store to get medicine.

After Joe took the medicine, he wanted to watch a movie. Dad said it was fine. (It was now 2:30 a.m.) Dad and Joe began the movie, and Mom, shaking her head at Dad in disbelief, went back to sleep. At 4:00 a.m., when the movie was over, Joe wanted to play. Dad said he should get some sleep, but Joe cried and whined, so he and Dad played cars for a while. Finally, at 5:00 a.m., Dad put Joe in bed because he got an emergency call and had to leave for work.

Joe was tired the next day, and so was Dad. Joe's sore throat got worse instead of better.

Every family can decide if they need to establish bedtime rules for sick children or not. The parents can discuss situations like this and have a tentative plan in mind. Common sense says Joe needs sleep in order to get well.

I have counseled many families where the children have been given too much power. In a situation like this, Joe is not old enough to have good judgment. Parents need to be responsible for making these kinds of decisions when children are young.

However, I always like to give children a choice. Decision-making is a skill that is beneficial to all of us and beginning early can give children confidence. Joe needs to go back to bed at 2:00 a.m., but he can make other choices:

* Shall I sleep with my teddy bear or my bunny?
* Do I want the nightlight on or off?
* Will the door be open or shut?

Joe is old enough to make daily choices like this. Give him a chance to make some selections, such as what he will wear, what music he wants to listen to, and which toys he wants to play with.

Family meetings are an excellent place for Joe to begin to learn how to make decisions, a place for the family to work together. They are a venue for parents to plan together for the good of themselves and their children. Remember, a democracy doesn't allow us to do anything we want.

Democracy is limited freedom with choices.

BALANCING POWER IN RELATIONSHIPS

Healthy marriage relationships have a fairly equal balance of give and take. In our society, egalitarianism has replaced male dominance of a bygone age. However, the equilibrium can be thrown off-kilter by many issues, such as addictions or affairs. If one of the partners develops a problem, the marriage can become disabled. I counseled many couples struggling with issues such as this. If one, or both, of the people involved has a strong sense of self, the relationship has a chance to survive. If there are children, as I have said before, it's especially important to at least try to salvage the marriage.

This is the story of one couple I worked with.

Liam worried about his wife, Emma. She spent too much time on the computer. He had a gut feeling that she was gambling again, this time on the internet. He had moved his family from Las Vegas two years ago to keep her out of the casinos. Luckily his internet marketing business didn't care where he lived.

Liam needed to confront Emma, but he hated to do it. He wanted to believe everything was OK. He had tried to check the credit card balance, but the password had been changed, and he couldn't get into the account.

He went to the credit union the next day and put a stop on the card.

That afternoon, when he left his office in the back of the house, Emma was waiting for him outside the door. "There's something wrong with the credit card. I can't get it to go through."

"Are you buying something online?" he asked.

"Yes, uh . . . I found a good price on shoes for Jackson." Emma turned her body away from Liam. "Y-you know how he's grown the last few months."

Liam's heart dropped to the pit of his stomach. She wasn't telling him the truth. "I'll take him to get shoes tonight."

Emma faced him. "But I need you to take care of the problem with the credit card."

"I've got a big job I'm in the middle of. I'll sort the card out in a day or two."

Emma's jaw tightened. "No, I need it tonight."

"Why?" asked Liam. "What's so urgent?"

"Oh, you'd never understand."

"Try me."

"Fine." She clenched her fists. "If you need to know, I'm playing a little again."

He felt sick. "I had a feeling."

"I'm not going to quit for you or the kids this time."

"But it's not good for the kids to see you on the computer all the time."

Emma put her hands on her hips. "I know that . . . I'm thinking of . . ."

Liam looked at her, waiting to see if she had anything in mind.

"I need my own space. I'm moving out. I just can't worry about the kids or have you breathing down my neck all the time."

"Please don't leave us," Liam begged. "The kids need you. I need you. If you stay, the kids don't have to know what's happening."

"Just pay for my apartment for a couple of months. I may decide to come back. But for now I need to get away." She looked at the floor. "My job at city hall will cover my other expenses."

Liam sighed. "How are we going to tell the children?"

"You tell them after I've left," said Emma. "I don't want to face crying kids hanging around my neck."

"You'll feel too guilty," Liam shot back.

Emma turned to leave. "Maybe. I'll pack my things and be gone by dinner."

Liam's heart sank. The knot in his stomach felt like it filled his whole gut. Emma left.

That night Liam and the children sat down to pizza.

Liam dished salad onto everyone's plate. "We might as well have a family council while we eat. I have something to tell you."

"Where's Mom?" asked Harper, age 6.

"It's about Mom," said Ella, age 10. "I saw her packing her suitcase this afternoon."

"Is she leaving us?" asked Harper.

"Yes," said Jackson, age 15. "I'll bet she's gambling again."

"She can't," said Ella. "We don't live in Vegas anymore."

"You can gamble online," said Jackson.

Tears slipped down Harper's cheeks. "The other kids at school have Moms that stay home. Why can't my mom?"

Liam hung his head. "You all know about it, and I haven't said anything."

"It's not like we're stupid," said Jackson, "or blind. We live here too, you know."

The children all knew what was happening without Liam saying a word. They'd been through the trauma of Mom's addiction before when they moved from Las Vegas.

Liam cancelled their credit cards, opened a bank account for Emma's rent money, and changed their joint account to be in his name only. He hated doing it, but he had to protect the rest of his money. There was still a big debt to pay from her Las Vegas gambling. He couldn't afford any more drain on his account.

After Emma had been gone for two weeks, she came home one afternoon for a visit." I missed the children," she told Liam.

What about me? wondered Liam.

Jackson was angry with his mom and refused to see her. Ella begged her to stay home. Harper clung to her and cried.

Liam's chest felt tight. Maybe she'll stay, he thought. He told Emma she could come home if she'd quit gambling. She refused. Desperate, he pleaded again. She wouldn't quit.

Liam and the children had been in therapy with me in Las Vegas for only a few months before he decided to move. I told him a geographic fix for the problem wouldn't work, but he wanted to try it. He asked me to recommend a therapist in his new city. He found a new counselor and a codependency group.

Liam kept in touch with me once in a while to let me know how things were going. His codependency group helped him see that he needed to let Emma go. For now, he had to realize that he was a single parent, raising three children on his own. He and the kids could pull together and be a happy family.

He learned these rules about relationships:

The person whose behavior is most deviant has the power.

Emma's deviant behavior (gambling) disrupted the entire family, causing stress and anxiety for every member.

The person who wants the relationship the least has the most power.

Emma also wanted the relationship the least, so she had double power.

Six months went by. Liam and the children got along fine. They discussed their weekly schedules and worked out a job chart in family council. The nights got lonely, so they added a game night once a week. All of them enjoyed laughing and playing together.

Emma maxed out her credit cards and lost her job. Liam still gave her money for her apartment, but she couldn't pay the utilities. She had nowhere to go. Emma had 'bottomed out,' and she wanted to come home.

By this time Liam was strong enough to tell her she had to make some changes. Emma was willing. She found her own therapist and attended Gamblers Anonymous meetings. She found another job and made arrangements to be responsible for her debts.

Notice that the balance of power has shifted. Emma wanted the relationship now, and so did Liam—if Emma let go of her addiction.

Family relationships had been damaged and would take some time to repair. Jackson was still angry and blamed his mother. While Emma was gone, Ella spent a lot of time at her best friend Sally's house. She loved Sally's mother. Ella considered her the kind of a mother she wanted. Harper clung to Emma. She panicked if Emma went to the store alone. Harper was sure she would leave again.

This family had a lot of healing to do. Years have now passed. Liam and Emma resurrected their marriage. They both would tell you they are stronger because of their problems. The children are grown, and all three have made peace with their mother. At age 29, Jackson isn't married yet, and he will tell you he's very fussy about the kind of girls he dates. Ella is friends with her mother, but if she has a problem, she talks things over with Sally's mom first. Harper loves her mother and spends as much time with her as she can.

An addiction can devastate a family. The effects are far-reaching, but humans are resilient and able to heal.

If people are willing to work on their relationships, they can most likely be saved.

When Emma left, notice that everyone in the family, including the children, knew that their mother was gambling again.

The definition of a family secret is something that everyone knows, but nobody talks about.

Think about your own family. Do you have issues that everyone knows about that you never discuss? At times, every family has a few. Hopefully you can learn to talk about your secrets. It takes the power out of them to be able to discuss them.

As Liam attended his support group and went to therapy, he became stronger, and so did the children. They used their family council each week to talk about their feelings and organize themselves to carry on without their mother. Until Emma lost everything, she wasn't willing to change. Emma could see that Liam and the children were OK on their own. That was part of her losing everything.

Healing after an addiction is difficult for everyone, but it can be done. It takes time to rebuild trust. Notice that Jackson is still distrustful of relationships. He has some fear about marriage. Ella found a substitute relationship that works for her. She and her mother have repaired their connection, but when Ella really needs to talk, she goes to Sally's mother. Harper is still clinging to her mother in some fashion—still trying to heal the hurt she felt as a young child when her mother abandoned her.

As a side note, remember that Liam executed a geographic fix when Emma began gambling in Las Vegas. He felt if he just left the area, everything would be fine. The problem is that geographic fixes almost never work because they don't address the root of the problem. Emma had some internal deficits that she needed to heal in order to recover from the addiction. Since those issues were not addressed, she went back to her gambling.

Family councils facilitated the healing in this family. Obviously they needed outside intervention in order to reinvent themselves, but meeting together and talking did the following:

* Provided everyone greater insight into the problems
* Helped the family be solution-focused
* Allowed the children to share their feelings
* Gave Liam a chance to support his children by listening to their feelings

> "Scars are not injuries . . . A scar is healing. After injury, a scar is what makes you whole."
>
> —CHINA MIÉVILLE

When Faced with Special Circumstances

Children with Asperger's Syndrome

Family councils can be an important vehicle in helping a family work together with special needs kids. Helping children in a family understand special needs characteristics, set boundaries, and talk through feelings can assist in normalizing difficult relationships.

A friend shared her arduous situation with me. She and her husband raised six children forty years ago. One of them had what they now diagnose as Asperger's syndrome before there was even a name for his disorder.

My friend could tell by the time Baker was two years old that he was different. He shied away from other children, never involving himself in the group. When he ran outside to play, he often stumbled and fell. He was socially inept, unable to relate to his siblings and other children in the neighborhood. He focused on minute details of intricate subjects such as atomic weights and spent every waking minute studying these subjects.

Often Baker sat in the middle of the living room floor and rocked back and forth, yelling out complaints and advice to his family. According to him, everyone was doing everything wrong.

His behavior was erratic. He yelled, hit his siblings, and never understood cause and effect. His older sisters were afraid of him. His younger brothers felt embarrassed. Baker wandered the house in the middle of the night, scaring the other children in their beds.

He lived disconnected from everyone and everything. In school he just sat there. He didn't qualify for special education classes because he wasn't a problem. At recess he stood near the corner of the building and seldom interacted with others.

One teacher said there was nothing wrong with Baker. His mother should quit comparing him to his older sister. Another teacher said Mom was to blame for his antisocial behavior. She should involve him in more activities.

Mom took Baker to a doctor at a prestigious medical hospital. The doctor said there were no facilities in the state to help a child like Baker. She should just do the best she could.

In spite of Baker's problems, his parents loved him, and the members of his church cared about him.

When Baker was sixteen, the family moved to a new area, and they found a psychiatrist who told Mom she had done everything right. Baker functioned at a higher level than most kids with his disorder. By this time the disorder had a name—Asperger's syndrome.

Mom felt a huge weight lifted off her shoulders for the first time since Baker was a baby. His problems weren't her fault. She had done something right. She had good medical support and someone who would listen to her frustration.

What a difficult trial this family went through.

Baker is now in his forties. He has held a job and raised a daughter. At the present time, he is on disability because of multiple health problems, but he's happy with his life.

How could family councils have helped this situation? Let's remember the purpose of a family council:

The purpose of a family council is to help the family pull together.

Did Baker's family need to pull together? Absolutely. Parents and children need to support each other. It had to be frightening for Baker's siblings to grow up with him. They never knew if they were going to get a lecture or get punched in the gut. I'm sure everyone in the family worried when Baker roamed the house at night.

Families with special needs kids have to *talk, talk, talk* and *plan, plan, plan.* Use the family council structure as a resource to open up communication.

My friend said that she didn't really know what her other children were thinking or how they felt about Baker. As adults her children talk about it now, but when they were young, there was no forum to discuss their feelings.

Use a family council to find out what your children think. Help your kids talk about tough situations like this.

There is more information and support for families with special needs children now than there was forty years ago. No one has to experience quite what this family went through. It was traumatic for everyone in the family not to have resources, including Baker.

How can a family with special needs children become synergistic? The following is a list of things that will work for all children with special needs, not just Asperger's.

* Study all you can.
* Use your community resources.
* Understand the research in the field.
* Include the children in your quest for information.
* Talk about feelings and how to handle difficult situations.
* Have everyone share their knowledge with the family, their classmates, and friends.
* Use the family council to support each other and your special child.

> "Someone I loved once gave me a box full of darkness. It took me years to understand that this, too, was a gift."
>
> —MARY OLIVER

CHILDREN WITH DOWN SYNDROME

We have a Down syndrome child, Tia, age 14, in our extended family. She spreads love like a glowing beacon of light. Everyone is enriched by her presence. She is a blessing to us all and as cute as any child could be—although very stubborn.

Her mother (our niece) has five children, with Tia right in the middle. Tia's family holds family council meetings when they have something important to discuss—vacations, deciding bedroom changes, planning family activities, etc.

Tia stays for family meetings if she is having a good day. Sometimes she is focused on what the family is discussing, and sometimes she has other ideas in her head. At one family council, she was planning her marriage to Donny Osmond, and that was all she could talk about, so she chose not to attend that meeting.

In an earlier meeting, Tia gave good suggestions about what activities she wanted to do on their summer vacation.

This family is caring and accepting of Tia, and Tia loves everyone. She is mainstreamed into her junior high, and one of her goals is to greet students and teachers politely with her words and a handshake (but not hug or kiss them) as she walks down the school corridors.

Family councils have been a good place for the parents to ask for the older children's help with Tia—to read to her, play with her, and help her do her weekly chores. The meetings are a good place for the kids to share their feeling about setting boundaries and having some private time of their own.

> "Sometimes I need only to stand wherever I am to be blessed."
>
> —MARY OLIVER

CHILDREN WITH FETAL
ALCOHOL SYNDROME

Children with fetal alcohol syndrome have very poor impulse control. They can be difficult to handle, and consistent family boundaries are important to help a child with this diagnosis function as well as can be expected in the real world.

Marilyn, a single mother with two children, holds her family councils on an informal weekly basis. Her son Burt, age 8, is always present at the meeting and is very good at being solution-focused.

Marilyn and her ex-husband adopted their child, Ellen, age 6, who came to them through foster care and has fetal alcohol syndrome. Ellen has a difficult time focusing on the task at hand and is easily distracted. Sometimes she comes to family meetings and stays only a few minutes, and Marilyn can tell whether Ellen will be able to center herself on the discussion or not. If Ellen is unable to give her attention to the planning, her mother waits to meet with Burt until Ellen is in bed. If Marilyn doesn't handle the meetings this way, Ellen is so disruptive they can't get anything done.

When Marilyn and Burt meet later, they not only hold a planning meeting, but they also discuss Burt's frustration with Ellen when she destroys his projects, like his latest model airplane. They brainstorm to decide how to protect Burt's things.

If you have a special needs children living in your home, you will know the best way to involve them in your family council. Do what works for all of you. If the children's needs are not being met at the council, find them another activity while the rest of the family is together. If the children aren't disruptive and can participate, include them in the meeting. If your special needs children can't attend to what's going on, keep them with the rest of the family but give them an activity of their own.

> "I know God will not give me anything I cannot handle. I just wish He wouldn't trust me with so much."
>
> —MOTHER TERESA

ELDERLY FAMILY MEMBERS

When our children were younger—in grade school and middle school—my maternal grandmother Nana, age 97, came to live with us (see Introduction). She had been in my mother's care for years, but as she got older, she couldn't be left alone during the day. She once made cookies and left them in the oven until they burned to a crisp, smoking up the house. Another time, she went out into the yard to work in her rose bed and fell. So she came to live with us.

We had to make some adjustments in our family to accommodate her. Family council was the place we discussed the changes that needed to be made. Bedroom adjustments were decided, and toys had to be picked up at all times because Nana could trip over something on the floor she didn't see.

The kids came up with the idea of a clutter hunt. We rotated who was in charge of the hunt each week. That person's job was to check the house before they left for school, just before dinner, and in the evening when everyone was ready for bed. Any stray clothing, books, or toys were put in a laundry basket, and family members could buy their lost items back for ten cents. The money was put in a jar and saved for a party.

It only took a week or two before everyone remembered to pick up their things off the floor so Nana would be safe.

We organized Nana's care at family council. Our oldest daughter loved to do Nana's hair each week. Our children took turns changing her bed, painting her nails, and reading books to her. Our son loved to play checkers with Nana. She enjoyed sitting on the patio and watching the kids in the swimming pool. She shuffled her walker out to the garden daily to see how the peas and tomatoes were doing.

She brightened up at family council because she thought my husband was her old boyfriend from grade school. She wanted her name put on the job chart, and she volunteered to fold all the socks and underwear. My husband chuckled each morning when he got a clean pair of socks out of the drawer. They were always mismatched.

Several weeks later at a family meeting, the kids decided they had earned enough money from the clutter hunt to go to the Science Center. The kids—especially our oldest daughter—wanted to take Nana with us instead of getting a sitter because she had earned the trip as well.

I reminded them that she would probably not remember the next day that she'd been on the outing, but they wanted to take her anyway. Everyone had fun at the museum pushing her around in the wheelchair, and they thought it great to go to the head of the line because we had a handicapped person in our party.

Our oldest daughter spent a lot of extra time with Nana, explaining the exhibits and making sure she understood each concept. It is a precious memory of mine and also of our oldest daughter's. She was so sweet with Nana. (And no, Nana didn't remember the trip the next day.)

Nana lived in our home for two years and died just several months before her 100th birthday. It was a blessing to have her with us.

At every family council, we talked about how to keep the family functioning smoothly and care for Nana's needs. As we discussed each problem that arose, our children learned these values:

* Patience as they watched the process of senility and aging
* Love as they served her

* Understanding as we talked about stories from her childhood
* Compassion as they shared their lives and their fun with her

The privilege of caring for her was a gift that has continued to fill our family with love and compassion long after her death, and family councils were the glue that kept us functioning smoothly.

> # "It is in the shelter of each other that people live."
>
> —*IRISH PROVERB*

CHAPTER 4:

Nurturing Messages for Your Children

Affirmative messages have great power in relationships. We communicate in a family on many levels. It is a challenge to keep positive energy flowing, but the rewards of doing so will bring greater goodness and blessings into our lives than we can ever imagine.

Family councils are a great vehicle for establishing this kind of ambience in our homes.

"I AM IMPORTANT."

Family Councils are a good way to give children the message that they matter and are vital to the group. As you talk with your children, include them in decisions and listen to their opinions. They will come to know their worth by the way you relate to them. These meetings are a pivotal place to create and fulfill goals.

Here is the story of one family.

Mom and Dad sat in the porch swing. The cool summer night air wafted over them. They rocked gently to the sound of serenading crickets. With four kids—Mia, age 10; Gavan, age 8; Gabriel, age 6; and Alexis, age 4—it was rare that the couple got to spend time together, so this was a great time for them to talk about their family and set a plan.

Mom shifted in her seat. "Gabriel has had several temper tantrums this week."

Dad looked down at her. "He has had a couple, hasn't he?"

"Sometimes I see him as caught right in the middle of the kids—an older sister who is the star of everything, an older brother who is a great math whiz, and a baby sister that everyone adores."

Dad chuckled, "What's not to love about that little curly blond bundle of energy?"

"I just think Gabriel needs a self-esteem boost." Mom sighed.

"So what's the solution, Doc?" Dad squeezed her.

Mom kissed his cheek. "I've been thinking . . . it's Gabriel's turn to conduct family council this week. Maybe we could make it a special night for him. How about we put together a 'Who Am I' poster like we made for his school last year?"

"Great," said Dad. "What do you want me to do?"

"I'll go in right now and send some pictures to be printed at the store. You could pick them up on your way home after work tomorrow."

"Consider it done," said Dad.

"I'll have Mia make up a little song for him, and maybe Gavan could play a game of catch with him before dinner. Alexis can help me make his favorite chocolate chip cookies."

"This is all well and good," said Dad, "but one night isn't going to fix everything."

"We haven't done parent-child date nights for a while," said Mom. "I'll take him to the dinosaur museum. He loves that."

"Great idea," said Dad. "I'm glad we've had this conversation. I need to play catch with him a couple of nights a week myself."

Mom glanced up at Dad. "I get what you're saying. The spotlight and date night are good, but it's the little things we do daily that will make a difference." She sighed. "Sometimes I just scoot him off to bed before I rock Alexis to sleep. Maybe I can spend a little more time with him each evening."

"I call this a great planning meeting," said Dad. "Let's do it more often."

All of us require times of accountability. This parental goal-setting session was informal, but it helped both adults focus on the importance of a family problem and how to correct it. The family council may be the catalyst for change in this family, but it's the daily parental actions that will really make the difference.

> ## "Love me when I least deserve it because that's when I really need it."
>
> —SWEDISH PROVERB

"I CAN TAKE CARE OF MY SURROUNDINGS."

Family councils can be formal or informal. Sometimes problems arise that lend themselves to teaching moments. Wise parents will be able to use both formal and informal settings to augment children's understanding of their world. Parents will also teach them respect for their own personal property and the property of those around them.

Kevin and Karter, age 5, were twins. What one didn't think of, the other one did. Both boys were excited because the neighbor over their back fence was digging a swimming pool. The boys stood on patio chairs so they were tall enough to peer over the fence and watch the heavy equipment scoop away the dirt. When the hole was dug, a cement truck pulled into the neighbor's drive way. The boys squealed when a big tube shot the cement into the depression like a gun before the plasterers smoothed and shaped the cement.

It rained the next day, so there was no work on the pool. Kevin and Karter stood on the chairs to see if water had collected in the pool. It had. Kevin ran to the garden and picked up a rock. He pitched it over the fence, and it landed in the pool water with a plop. The boys giggled and ran to get more rocks.

"This is fun," said Karter.

Mother opened the sliding door to the patio and walked toward them. "What are you guys doing?"

Both boys looked at each other. "Nothing."

Mother turned over their hands and found rocks held in each one. "You were probably going to throw these."

Kevin dropped his on the patio and dusted his hands off on his pants. "Come on, Karter, let's go play trucks."

Karter jumped off his chair. "OK."

"Wait a minute," said Mother. "We need to talk."

Both boys looked at her.

"I'll bet it's been fun to watch that pool being dug. Is there any water in it from the rain last night?" She peeked over the fence. "I can see a few rocks in the bottom. What kind of noise did they make when they splashed into the water?"

"It was great, Mother," said Karter. "Want to hear what it sounds like?"

Mother bent down and looked into the boys' eyes. "The workmen will have to clean the rocks out before they can finish the pool. How would you like it if someone threw rocks in our pool?"

"Not good," said Kevin.

"Who would clean it up?" asked Mother.

Karter hung his head. "We couldn't swim until we got the rocks out."

"Sorry," said Kevin.

"Let's walk around and tell Mr. Jones you're sorry," said Mother. "I just made some cookies. We'll take him some."

At the next family council, the family discussed caring for their property and treating the neighbors' things with as much care as they did their own. The boys said they would protect other people's belongings.

Lessons like this are learned slowly—a little at a time. Several months later, the boys broke another neighbor's garage window by throwing rocks over the fence again. At family council, the boys realized they needed to buy a new window for the neighbor. After the twins worked for several weeks to pay the debt, they decided rock throwing was not a good idea—at least for now.

"I HAVE BOUNDARIES IN MY LIFE."

Boundaries can take many forms in our lives. They are associated with our relationships with others, and respect for others' rights and property. Parents also set boundaries in disciplining children and establishing parameters, like maintaining respect for the personal space of others, as is discussed in the following story. Any time an adult or child says "stop" to another person, they have set a boundary.

Personal interaction can be difficult and downright annoying if those around us don't respect our boundaries—like when they touch without permission or talk too loudly.

Family councils can be a means of finding solutions to boundary problems.

Luke's father abandoned him when he was a tiny baby. Luke's mother tried repeatedly to stay off drugs but couldn't, so Luke was placed in foster care. He'd been moved from home to home because he had poor impulse control and families found him bothersome to deal with.

Luke was now eight, and the courts had finally found a permanent home for him—his Aunt Bea and Uncle Dylan would raise him. They had three children of their own: Asher, age 10; Piper, age 12; and Addy, age 13.

The first few days after Luke came to live with his aunt and uncle, he kept to himself. But as he got used to the family, he began to tease and tickle his cousins—even after the kids asked him to stop. He stood too close to them when he talked, and his voice was a little too loud.

Aunt Bea called the social worker, wondering what to do about the situation. The social worker asked if she could meet with the family to give them some suggestions. Aunt Bea invited her to their next family council.

"That's a great place to discuss this problem," said the social worker.

Later that week the social worker met with the family. "What are your concerns?" she asked.

Addy glanced at Luke. "What do I do when I don't like someone touching me and tickling me even after I tell them to stop?"

"Good question." The social worker moved to the couch to sit next to Luke and Aunt Bea. "You been having trouble keeping your hands to yourself, Luke?"

Luke hung his head and nodded.

The social worker patted Luke's knee. "That's one of the goals Luke is working on with his therapist. How about we set up a signal everyone can use when someone is tickling or touching them against their wishes?"

"Good idea," said Aunt Bea, her arm around Luke.

The social worker looked at the children. "Everyone has different ideas for a signal. Sometimes kids use words, like saying, 'personal space.' And other times they have a sign, like pointing their thumbs down."

"Let's do a thumbs-down," said Luke.

"I think saying 'personal space' is a good idea," said Asher. "I want to be able to tell someone when I don't like what's happening."

"How does everyone else feel?" asked Uncle Dylan.

"Why don't we use both?" said Addy. "That way Luke has a signal, and those of us who want to can say our feelings."

The family voted for both words and a signal.

"Are there any other problems?" asked the social worker.

"I have a question," said Addy. "I feel uncomfortable when some-one stands too close to me when they're talking."

Piper nodded. "I agree. I think we should stand an arm's length away from another person when we want to talk to them."

"That's pretty far," said Uncle Dylan. "Sometimes I want to stand a little closer than that."

"How about from your hand to your elbow?" asked Addy.

"That would work," said Piper.

"Do you think you can remember that?" Aunt Bea asked Luke.

"I don't know," said Luke. "What if I mess up?"

"It's OK," said Piper. "None of us are perfect."

"We'll all try to remember, too," said Asher.

"We'll use our words and the signal," said Uncle Dylan.

Everyone voted to try it the next week.

The social worker slipped off the couch and knelt down in front of Luke. "What's your last goal?"

Luke sighed. "Talking too loud." He shrugged his shoulders. "I have a hard time remembering."

"How about we vote to just speak in whispers this week?" said Addy. "All of us."

"That's pretty soft," said Piper.

"I think it would be fun," said Uncle Dylan. "Just for the week, let's see if we can do it. I'll try."

They all voted to whisper and see how it went. They began their whispering week right after family council while they got out the milk and cookies for dessert.

This family was very supportive of Luke. Maybe he had just learned some bad habits at the foster homes. Maybe he felt inadequate and lonely and needed extra attention. And maybe he had some impulsiveness because he was exposed to drugs so early in life. As time goes along, the mental health system would sort out these problems. With the help of his therapist and this loving family, he had a chance of becoming a healthy, functional adult.

Setting boundaries can be an important function of family council.

There are many ways to set boundaries with children. Some families are very structured with set, unyielding rules. Other families are much more casual, working with fluid boundaries. The incidents we discussed in Chapter 2 about rule-setting will give you ideas for how you want to structure your family.

Choose the method that works best for your family. But whatever you decide, be predictable so children know what to count on.

Children need consistent fences.

"I AM A PROBLEM-SOLVER."

One of the greatest gifts we can give our children is to teach them to find solutions to obstacles that come their way. Every one of us will encounter troubles in our lives—it's just the way of human existence. But to be able to find resolution and allow the trials in our lives to strengthen us is a learned gift that takes practice.

In the following instance, the children called a family council meeting themselves to solve their problem.

Brittany, age 8, came home from school one day, scratching the back of her head.

"It really itches," she said.

"She may have lice," said Barbara, age 10. "Some of the other kids at school have it."

"Oh, no!" Mom parted the hair on the back of Brittany's neck. "I can see little bugs. You've got lice."

"What does that mean?" asked Brittany.

"That you don't wash your hair often enough," said Barbara.

"Not true," said Mom. "I've heard that lice pass from person to person rather easily. You could have picked up the bugs from other kids at school." Mom sighed. "I will not have lice roaming my house. I need to call the doctor's office to see about medication to get rid of them."

Brittany slumped in a kitchen chair.

Mother washed her hands. "I think we'll need to throw away all of your stuffed animals. These annoying little bugs live in pillows and the like."

"No," said Brittany. "Not my stuffed animals."

"Yes, all your animals must go," said Mom.

"We really don't know anything about lice for sure," said Barbara.

"Yeah." Brittany hugged her sister. "We don't know anything, so let's check the internet."

Barbara pushed Brittany away. "Don't touch me. I don't want those pesky things."

Brittany did an internet search for lice and found that all her sheets and towels and clothes needed to be washed in hot water. The carpets and furniture should be vacuumed. "Look," she said to Barbara, "stuffed animals can be dry-cleaned or put in an airtight bag for two weeks."

"Let's tell Mom," said Barbara.

"Woo-hoo!" Brittany raised her arms in victory.

They told Mom.

"Now, wait a minute," said Mom. "You can't trust everything you find on the internet."

"But this is written by a doctor," said Brittany.

"I don't know," said Mom.

Dad walked in the door from work. "Having a powwow?"

"As a matter of fact . . ." Mom's voice trailed off.

"I'm calling a family council," said Brittany.

"Right now?" asked Dad. "I haven't even taken off my shoes yet."

"Take them off," said Barbara. "Brittany needs a meeting."

The girls and Mom explained the situation to Dad.

"I just can't give up my stuffed animals," said Brittany. "I've had some of them since I was a baby."

"Maybe this is a blessing in disguise." Dad chuckled and smiled at Mom. "Your bed's piled so high with those toys you hardly have room to sleep there as it is."

"Dad!" Brittany put her hand on her hip. "I need my animals."

"The information on the internet was written by a doctor," said Barbara.

Dad looked at Mom. "What can we do here?"

"If you don't believe the internet, check with Dr. Smith and see what he says," Brittany pleaded.

"I have to call the office anyway to see what kind of medicated shampoo is best," said Mom.

Brittany jumped up and clapped her hands. "Mom, I'll get your phone."

Mom called, and the girls waited. "Dr. Smith agrees with the internet article," said Mom.

"Great," said Brittany. "I'll get some garbage bags."

Mom sighed. "You'll need the vacuum to suck all the air out."

"Oh, yeah." Brittany was already on her way down the hall to her bedroom.

After two weeks in an airtight bag, Brittany's animal family was bug-free. Her solution-focused mentality saved her stuffed pets, but more importantly, these things also happened:

* Both sisters worked together (including calling a family council) to solve the problem.
* Brittany had confidence in herself—enough to state her case.
* She followed through with a solution.
* When one idea didn't work, she found another that her parents could live with.

> # "It is not about problems; it is about solutions."
>
> ## —MARTIN HUNTER

"I CAN NEGOTIATE."

When our children were young, our family council decided on one hour of "free television" a day. The kids each chose one show, but they could also watch each other's programs. This set off a volley of negotiation. They met together and poured over the TV guide to make sure all their favorite broadcasts were chosen.

There was a lot of give and take in this process.

"I'll choose *Wonderful World of Disney*," said Kirsten.

"Then I'll take *Little House on the Prairie*," said Laura.

"I want *Carol Burnett*," said Robin, "so who will choose *Wild Kingdom*?"

"Maybe we can get Rebekah to pick that one," said Kirsten.

"She won't," said Laura. "She likes *The Smurfs*."

"Maybe we can talk Chris into *Wild Kingdom*," said Robin.

"He's only two. He's too little to choose," said Kirsten.

And so went the negotiations.

As you can see, there were more shows they wanted to watch than there were kids, so they came up with an idea. At family council they suggested they could read to earn extra television time (they knew that would go over well because we are all definitely reading advocates). So they voted to read an hour to earn an hour of TV time. We soon had a household of devoted readers. And, as time went on and they grew up, the reading became much more important than the television.

The children learned through our family council not only to negotiate with each other, but to negotiate with us, the parents. It is a skill they continue to use in their adult lives today—whether directing a classroom, business, library, sales force, or family of children, they use the skill of negotiating every day. It's a valuable gift to give your children.

"I AM SOLUTION-FOCUSED."

What a great opportunity we have to raise our children to become solution-focused. As we have already seen, family counsels are a great place to solve problems. But we can also teach children to keep trying if they don't succeed the first time.

Angela, age 15, loved to have her friends over after school during the week and invite them for a movie night on Friday or Saturday.

Taggart, age 13, complained that he never got a chance to entertain his friends because Angela's crowd was always there. He put his name on the family council agenda because he wanted a turn to have his own get-together.

"I want to have a party this Friday night," said Taggart.

"No fair," said Angela. "I've already invited kids over."

"It's my turn," said Taggart.

"I have an idea," said Angela. "All our friends can come. It'll be like a double party."

"I still want my own movie time," said Taggart. "We don't want to watch some sappy chick flick."

"I promise we won't," said Angela. "It'll be blast to have lots of kids over."

"Are you sure you want to do that?" asked Dad. "There could be problems with so many people here."

"You have to clean everything up after it's over," said Mother.

"We will," promised Angela.

The family voted to have combined parties.

On Friday night, the living room was so crowded with boys that Angela and her friends couldn't find a place to sit. They had to take the floor. When they went to get food, the boys had eaten all the pizza. To top it off, the boys started an army movie that the girls didn't like. The girls finally settled in Angela's bedroom, but the boys complained that their music was too loud.

After the party was over and the boys had gone home, Angela and her friends began to pick things up. She looked for Taggart and found him asleep in his room. Should she wake him to help clean up? She decided not to because this was his first party.

The kitchen was a mess. The boys had had an ice cream fight and slopped it all over the cabinet and floor. She and her friends complained to each other but mopped up since Angela had promised Mother.

"Next time Taggart can have his own party and clean up after himself," Angela said to her friends.

Angela didn't say anything to Taggart. She put her name on the agenda for the next council meeting, deciding to talk about it then.

"I'd like to suggest we take turns having parties," she said when her name came up on the agenda.

"We don't need to do that," said Taggart. "It was fun to be together."

Mother and Dad glanced at each other knowingly.

Angela outlined the problems she and her friends had with the combined gathering.

"Oh," said Taggart. "I didn't even see any of that. Thanks for cleaning up."

"I don't want to do it again," said Angela.

"Maybe we'll eat outside," said Taggart. "I don't want to clean up a mess either."

"We're going to Megan's house next week," said Angela. "Have your party then."

The family voted to take turns with their parties.

It's great to let kids work out their own solutions. Mother and Dad knew there could possibly be problems, but they let the kids work it out. You can tell this family had a healthy pattern of communicating with each other because both Angela and Taggart listened to each other, worked together, and remained solution-focused.

Council meetings are a great time for trial and error. It's good for kids to try and fail and then try again, learning the lessons that will propel them to healthy adulthood.

> ## "If everyone is moving forward together, then success takes care of itself."
> —HENRY FORD

"I CAN HANDLE TOUGH SITUATIONS."

Children often come up against tough situations at school, on the playground, or on the sports field. Family council is a great place to talk about tough situations and how to handle them. It's good to role-play solutions to help boost confidence and teach diplomacy. Children can learn social skills, and the home is a great place to teach them.

Jameson, age 10, moved to a new school in third grade. The kids called him "skinny" and "albino hair" because his hair was white-blond. He didn't even know what "albino hair" meant. He came home from school very upset and told his mom and dad about it.

His parents held an informal family meeting and talked about finding good things to say about each one of the kids who had teased him.

"But I don't want to do that," said Jameson. "They were mean to me."

"Try it," Dad suggested. "It'll really confuse the boys. They won't know what to do, and that's the most fun of all."

"I guess." Jameson shrugged his shoulders.

Dad role-played with Jameson until he could think of positive things to say to every boy in the group at school.

The next day at recess, Jameson gave the boys the compliments he had practiced with his dad. The boys didn't know what to say. Jameson smiled to himself. Dad was right, he thought. During recess the boys asked Jameson to join their soccer game.

Jameson continued to make friends. He ended up being buddies with the guy who called him "albino hair."

Sometimes bullying is not solved this easily, but Jameson was an assertive kid to begin with and just needed some advice on how to handle the situation.

> "If you can't go around it, over it,
> or through it, you had better
> negotiate with it."
>
> —*ASHLEIGH BRILLIANT*

"I CAN SET GOALS."

Methods of helping children set goals will be as varied as the young people involved. Family councils can help tailor the experience so that each child will be successful. Some kids are steady and consistent in their work, and others are enthusiastic at first but lose interest as time goes along. Teach all of your children to finish what they start.

Mitchell, age 10, had a reputation in the family for getting excited about a new project and then dropping it after a few weeks. The school hired a new after-school care leader who offered a guitar class. Mitchell really wanted to join the class, but he didn't have a guitar. His parents said they would rent one for him if he would practice every day. Dad brought the new instrument home the next night after work.

Mitchell opened the guitar case. "I'll practice an hour every night."

"That's too long," said Mother. "You'll start out spending a lot of time on it, but you won't keep that up. I know you too well."

Mother was being fairly blunt here—more blunt than I'm comfortable with. Be careful not to label a child. Children grow and change. Give them a chance to prove themselves. As parents, we have a responsibility to teach them another way.

Mitchell lifted the guitar out of the case. "This is really cool. I promise I'll practice an hour. There's a new piece the teacher taught us today that I really want to learn."

Mother handed Mitchell a notebook. "Record how much time you practice each day."

"Sure." Mitchell took the notebook under his arm and strummed the guitar on his way to the bedroom.

Dad followed him down the hall. "How about we check up on your goals at family council?"

"Great." Mitchell practiced an hour and fifteen minutes the first night. Then next afternoon he didn't have time for guitar because he had a big social studies test the next day. The following afternoon he could only squeeze in forty minutes because he had baseball practice. He missed the next two days.

At family council he showed the notebook to Mother and Dad. "I really tried."

"I know," said Mother. "How about setting a specific time each day to practice?"

Mitchell thought for a moment. "After dinner every night."

"But that's when your favorite TV show is on," said Dad.

"I'll record it," said Mitchell.

"How long will you practice?" asked Mother.

"One hour," said Mitchell.

"You already tried that and it didn't work," said Mother. "You won't have that long some nights because of your homework."

"Half an hour, then," said Mitchell.

"Great," said Dad. "We'll check to see how you're doing next week."

It may have taken a few weeks for Mitchell to find a time that worked for him and to practice consistently. Maybe he wouldn't want to record his favorite TV show some nights, and he'd have to find another time. It was fine for him to try and fail and try again until he found what worked for him.

The big picture concept the parents are teaching their child here is not to play the guitar, but to become self-directing and goal-oriented. What a great gift to give a child! But it will probably take some time for the child to internalize it. Just keep working at it. Be consistent yourself, and your children will meet their goals.

Here are some suggestions for goal setting in family council:

* Set long-term goals.
* Adjust your daily short-term goals to match your long-term goals.
* Keep the goals realistic for the age and maturity of the child.
* Be consistent.
* Let the child reestablish goals that work for him or her.
* Set up a regular time of accountability.
* If you wish, use available electronic apps to aid consistency.

> ## "If you don't know where you are going, you'll end up someplace else."
>
> —YOGI BERRA

"I AM ACCOUNTABLE."

Family councils are not always the best place to solve personal problems. If a child is troubled about something, ask the child how he or she feels about discussing it at a family council and follow the child's lead.

Beth hated math because she had never been very good at it. And now that she was taking pre-algebra, she hated it even worse. She just didn't understand it. Besides, the teacher was old-fashioned and didn't know what he was talking about.

Beth got her first test back with a big, red letter D on it. I'll just drop it in the garbage can here in the classroom so Dad and Mom won't know, she thought, breathing a sigh of relief. The second test came back with a D-minus on it. She dropped that one in the garbage also.

That night at dinner, Dad asked, "How is pre-algebra coming?"

Beth sighed. "Oh, fine."

"How about we look at your grades on the website before family council tonight?" asked Dad. "We like to talk about goals at our meeting anyway."

Beth's head jerked toward Dad. "You don't need to do that. Besides, I don't think the grades are posted yet. And I *don't* want to talk about this at family council."

"Let's just check."

Beth knew she was toast. She got up from the table to help Mom with the dishes.

Mom smiled and put her arm around Beth. "Thanks, honey, but it's not your turn tonight. It's Jason's."

"Uh," said Beth, "I like to help. I'll just rinse the plates for him."

Dad walked up behind Beth. "Let's check your grades."

Beth clenched her fists. "You go check. I'll help Mom and Jason."

"Come on, Beth," said Dad. "Is it that bad?"

Beth nodded, and a tear slipped down her cheek. Dad pulled her close. "Let's go look. We can work it out."

"I just can't do math, Dad." She sighed. "And I don't want to talk about this at family council. Jason will just think I'm stupid."

Dad checked the grades. "Well, the D and D-minus need to change. Let's get a tutor for you."

"No, Dad, that's too embarrassing! Don't tell Mom and Jason."

"I want you to tell Mom after family council, but Jason doesn't need to know."

"Thanks, Dad."

Dad hugged her. "I know Mr. Taylor, the head of the math department at the high school. He'll help us find a high school student that can help you."

Beth covered her face with her hands. "I just can't do math."

"Yes, you can."

Beth and Dad told Mom about the grades that night after Jason had gone to his room.

Mr. Taylor recommended a girl that came every afternoon to help Beth. Day after day, she sat with Beth and explained the concepts. Day after day, Beth got better at understanding her math assignments. The next test she got a C. She was so excited that she raced home to show her tutor.

Beth's math scores improved steadily until she had B grades on her assignments.

Most of the time, family council is a place to discuss problems, but let the child have a say as to whether he or she wants to share a personal trial with everyone or not. Dad was wise to ask Beth to tell Mom, however. Both parents need to know. It's not OK to exclude one parent. Remember, the most important relationship in the family is between husband and wife. Beth did eventually tell Jason after she felt a little better about her progress, but not until she was ready.

Dad was paying attention as a parent in checking the grades. His big-picture goal was teaching accountability to Beth, and he did it in a kind, loving, nonconfrontational way.

Notice that Beth didn't like being accountable at first. In my experience, there's an accountability button that switches on in kids' brains somewhere between ages 12 and 16. It's different for every child, but it's a relief when they take responsibility for their actions (such as grades) so you, as a parent, don't have to monitor them.

None of us likes to admit our failures, but unless we look at them, we can't improve. Beth can now become the best that she can be.

Accountability is part of life for us all—whether with performance evaluations at work, peer reviews, school grades, or editorial critiques. Teaching this skill of accountability to young people, whether at family councils or elsewhere, is a valuable tool they'll use the rest of their lives.

> ## "The right thing to do and the hard thing to do are usually the same."
> ### —STEVE MARABOLI

"I HAVE A LOVING ATTITUDE."

The attitude of a child like the boy in the example below makes a huge difference in how he feels about himself and how he treats those around him. If he feels sorry for himself and has a chip on his shoulder, he's not going to be kind and loving. The boy in the following incident has reasons to feel his life hasn't been the best, but he also has reasons to think his life is great. Even though this family had been holding family councils, the meetings themselves hadn't changed his bad attitude. It took an outside force to help this child embrace love and caring.

We can all find the bad if we look for it, but we can also find the good around us. It all depends on where we search.

I saw this family in counseling for several problems. This is an isolated incident in their healing process.

Ferguson, age 12, felt angry inside. He kicked a stray soccer ball against the brick fireplace just as his mother walked in from work.

"Take the ball outside," she greeted him.

Ferguson shrugged, dropped his head, and pushed the ball into the corner. "I didn't break anything."

"Why can't you be happy?" asked his mother.

"My life is the pits," said Ferguson.

"It's not so bad," said his mother.

"You and Dad both have to work, so it's like I'm an orphan."

"You're not an orphan." His mother sighed. "You wanted to be at home by yourself when you turned twelve. Besides, we've had this conversation countless times before."

"That's because my life never changes." Ferguson grabbed a cookie from the jar.

"The new neighbors moved in next door," said Mother. "It looks like there's a boy your age. I saw him out playing basketball in the driveway when I drove in."

Ferguson toed his basketball out from under the laundry room table and headed out the door. He watched the movers unloading the van next door and bounced his ball twice in his own driveway.

The boy next door turned to face Ferguson.

Ferguson carried his ball across the lawn to the boy's driveway. "I'm Ferguson."

"Hey." The boy smiled. "I'm DeLoy."

"DeLoy?" Ferguson eyed him.

"Yeah, stupid name, isn't it?" DeLoy made a basket.

"Maybe," Ferguson mumbled, throwing the ball up and missing.

"I wish I could change it." DeLoy made another basket.

"You've just moved to a new place and no one knows your name. You can change it."

"To what? There's no nickname for DeLoy."

"How about just D?"

"That's cool, but what if someone asks what it stands for?" DeLoy dribbled behind his back and shot again. He missed.

"Tell them it's just D. No one will ever know." Ferguson shot and made it.

A woman came out of DeLoy's house, a little girl toddling behind her. "Ahhhh." She made a funny calling noise and then began to sign with her hands to DeLoy.

DeLoy glanced at Ferguson. "My mom's deaf. She's going to the store to get groceries with my little sister, DeLane."

Ferguson smiled. He reached out to shake DeLoy's mom's hand.

"His name is Ferguson," said DeLoy, signing as he talked.

"Pleased to meet you," said DeLoy's mom. The words didn't come out like normal speech, but he could still understand her.

DeLoy looked at her and said, signing back. "I don't want to come to the store."

Ferguson glanced at DeLoy. "Tell her you can stay and have dinner with me."

She signed to DeLoy again.

"Mom says I can stay at your house if she meets your mom and gets the OK from her."

The three of them went next door to Ferguson's house, D's little sister tagging along after them.

"Mother," said Ferguson, "this is D, our new neighbor, and his mom."

"Hello," said Mother.

D's mom smiled.

"Can D stay for dinner?" asked Ferguson.

"Sure," said Mother. "We'd love to have him. Tonight's family council. Do you want to ask him to stay for both?"

That night after dinner, the four of them met for family council—it was Dad's turn to conduct. After giving compliments and going over weekly responsibilities, Dad picked up the agenda. "Ferguson, looks like you name is first on the list. 'Phone' is written by your name."

"Yeah, Dad. I want to know when I can get a cell phone."

Dad glanced at Mother. "Your mother and I need to talk about it, but I would guess we'll decide to let you have one as soon as you can pay for it—when you're sixteen and can get a job."

"Just get a family plan," said Ferguson. "My phone will cost hardly any extra."

"We'll talk about it," said Dad, glancing at D.

"Besides, I could really use one now—all my friends have one. I can call you to let you know where I am. Think of the help that would be."

Mother turned to D. "What about you? Do you know when you'll get a phone of your own?"

D looked out the window. "Well, you could say the phone is already mine. I always have to answer it because my mom can't. She has a special typing phone that she uses when I'm at school, but all the rest of the time I have to talk and tell her what the person on the phone is saying."

"Do you get tired of it?" asked Ferguson.

"Sometimes."

"Your mom must be glad she has you to help her," said Mother.

"My mom relies on me a lot. I usually go shopping with her so I can talk to the store clerk. I read stories to my little sister every night because Mom can't. One day, some kids got into the backyard of our old house and were throwing rocks at our dog. She couldn't hear it, but I chased them away."

"Sounds like you take lots of responsibility at home." Dad glanced at Ferguson.

Ferguson ducked his head.

D smiled. "Yeah, I guess I do." He folded and unfolded his hands. "But I don't mind it. I love my mom and want to help her."

Ferguson looked at the ground. "Uh . . . Dad, forget the next item on the agenda, okay?"

Dad raised his eyebrows. "About making sure Mom has your laundry washed and folded on time?"

Ferguson blushed. "Yeah, forget it. . . . I guess I should help more."

Over the following weeks, the boys became friends. Ferguson learned that D's father had had an affair and left the family.

Ferguson sat in the kitchen one afternoon talking to his mother after she got home from work. "I guess my life is pretty good. I have a mother and a father that can both hear—and they live in the same house."

"Everyone comes from different circumstances." His mother handed him a bottle of juice. "When we look at other people's troubles, we find our own aren't so bad."

Slowly, Ferguson's attitude changed. He watched how D treated his mother and sister, and Ferguson's defiance lessened. Ferguson's background is complicated, and there were many other reasons he acted like a spoiled child with a bad attitude, but his friendship with D helped. Ferguson became more kind to and respectful of his parents and took more responsibility for himself.

Our outlook on life makes a huge difference. Sometimes it's helpful to watch those around us and adopt the good we see in them into our own lives.

We cannot give and receive love if we have a bad attitude. As Ferguson's insolence lessened, he learned about love.

Here are a few other things that this family discovered while in counseling:

* If we want to have loving relationships, we must model love.
* We need to talk with our children about feelings so they will learn empathy.
* Our children will learn about love when we give service as a family.
* We need to talk with our children about examples of love and service around us.

* If we give our children positive feedback, they will learn to be optimistic.
* Everyone needs at least four hugs per day.
* Caring for a pet can be a great way to teach children about love and service.

Family councils may have aided change for Ferguson, but the catalyst was an outside source, a neighbor boy. Alternative perspectives—good and bad—can come from many directions. Be aware of your child's environment and use your councils to help them understand the world around them and foster a healthy attitude.

> ## "Attitude is the little thing that makes a big difference."
>
> —WINSTON CHURCHILL

CHAPTER 5:

Learning, Playing, and Growing Together as Part of Family Council

One of the goals of families is to help children become the best they can be. The following ideas will aid your kids in building the skills they need to develop to their full potential. There seems to be a magic time during the formative years when children learn and gain proficiency much easier than they do as adults. For instance, children can learn to play the piano with great proficiency (if they practice) during their childhood and teen years. I have observed that adults who work to gain the same skills struggle and usually don't achieve the expertise that comes with youth. So help your children make the best of these formative years. Guide them to increase their talents.

Remember that family councils don't have to be just about solving problems, and they don't have to be only formal meetings. They can be extemporaneous activities with the overarching purpose of growing up together and loving each other.

❧ Learning Together ❧
Reading

Family councils are a wonderful time to read together. When our children were growing up, we loved reading each evening. In the summer, we read after lunch. We studied the Bible in the morning before school. Teach your children to love books—open up the world to them.

Informal family meetings are a good time to begin reading to your babies as they start to learn about their world. By the time they are toddling around, they will have a small speaking vocabulary and better picture recognition that will build as the years go by. Young ones love books with nursery rhymes and rhythm games—both will teach the child words and concepts.

Every kindergartner and first grader needs to practice reading. Spend some family time each night encouraging them to build their skills—and their self-esteem. Grade school kids love joke and riddle books. What a fun method to aid both reading and retention! Children enjoy retelling new jokes.

Study to gain new ideas and information. We have a grandson interested in snakes. His mother takes him to the library every week to check out new books about the reptiles.

Read after family council meetings for sheer pleasure, or spend a little more time enjoying a chapter together every night. Find a book that fits your children's age group and the genre they are interested in. I made it a practice to savor the Newberry books each year for a family activity. Find what works for you.

Because I read to our children, they read to our grandchildren. I love that. Your investment pays off a hundred fold—a lot better than the interest from your bank account. Formal and informal family councils pay great dividends.

Music and Art

The gift of self-expression through any artistic medium is important for a child's development. Let your young person establish his or her own path. Listen, and your child will follow the direction of his or her soul.

A mother allowed her teens to form a rock band. Members of her conservative church congregation were shocked that she would let her boys play that kind of music because some of the modern songs had such "bad words" and "terrible messages."

The family had a plan for that problem. At family council, the boys, with the approval of the parents, decided they would compose their own musical selections and only play those songs with clean, uplifting words. The boys are grown now and jam with each other and their friends once in a while when their professional duties allow them to be in town at the same time.

The boys learned much more than music during their teen years. They learned that they could express themselves as they wished. They were trusted. They were valued. And they could be part of a changing culture.

Family meetings are a great time to review an opera plot before you attend the performance. It saves you from reading the program notes and gives everyone a chance to ask all the questions they have. Study an artist's life before you see his or her works in a museum. These principles of planning an event and reading ahead of time will enhance all kinds of cultural events.

Our children loved to dress up and dance when they were little. Family councils are a great time to expose them to different kinds of music. Rhythm bands are lots of fun for little kids, and all you need are pots and spoons. Rap to the Three Billy Goats Gruff story and have them repeat "trip-trap" with you. Sing when they're on the swings in the park. Create fun family music activities wherever you go.

Have a family council concert. Fill glass jars with different levels of water and let the children tap them with a spoon. They can make up their own tunes or play songs they know.

If we'd had an especially busy week and the house was a disaster, we had a cleaning fest—with music, of course. Dusting and vacuuming to the beat gets the work done faster. Cleaning the bathrooms calypso style is fun for everyone.

Family meetings can become a performance night if the kids are getting ready for a piano recital or concert. Councils can be a time to rehearse musicals or simulate melodramas.

Be as creative with art projects and other family interests as you are with music—but, above all, enjoy exposing your children to the world around them. Savor the creations of the world. Inspire your children to be the best they can be.

> ## "For me, music-making is the most perfect expression of any emotion."
>
> —LUCIANO PAVAROTTI

> ## "A true work of art is but a shadow of the divine perfection."
>
> —MICHELANGELO

MONEY MANAGEMENT

Each family will handle money matters with children a little different-ly. Set your goals at family council and earn your way to success. Our children all had jobs to do because they were part of the family. But there was extra work they could complete to earn an allowance. A list of paying tasks hung on the fridge, and if anyone needed money, they could do any of those they wished. If they wanted more money, they could get a part-time job when they were old enough.

We opened bank accounts for our kids when they were in second grade because their teacher taught them about economics and money management. She set up a classroom store where each child had a booth filled with items they had made, like cookies, pom-pom animals, and decorative candles. They tabulated their earnings from their store and deposited their savings at a local bank. They learned basic banking skills in school, and we augmented that knowledge as a family.

After our children reached the age of 12, they paid half for extra things they wanted, like nail polish or a new video game.

Plan what you want to teach your children about money and move forward in that direction. Use family council as a venue to work out problems and ask for an accounting of each person's goals. Help your children be solution-focused enough to follow through with their ideas.

> "Earn all you can, save all you can, give all you can."
>
> —JOHN WESLEY

Connection with Your Ancestors

Many families keep scrapbooks and photo albums of grandparents and great-grandparents. Expand this idea by creating memories of your choice with art, videos, or audio recordings. For those who love to sew or do crafts, make a memory quilt or use other mediums such as clay, origami, or fabric painting.

Create a family crest. Do some research, find your old family crests, and combine them to make your own version. Construct one for your immediate family. Decide together what to put on it. Choose meaningful symbols to describe your family.

One of the most memorable family reunions we had was when we visited the birthplace of our ancestors. One of my great-grandfathers settled in a small Idaho town. It was a life-changing experience to visit. First, we saw the old family home that is now a museum. Then we toured a church building the immigrant Swiss brothers constructed as experienced stonemasons. As we brushed out hands over the cool rock, we knew this was the workmanship of their hands. As we walked the paths our ancestors walked and saw the same sunrises and sunsets, we came to know that family.

If you tell the stories about yourselves and your extended families, children know they are part of a larger group. They will feel connected to the past, giving them strength to face the challenges that come into their lives, according to Bruce Feiler (Emery University) who has done extensive research concerning children's resilience to problems.

Children love to know the crazy stories about holidays, vacations, big family get-togethers. Our kids laugh at the old story of an uncle, spaced out on prescription drugs, who drove the back hoe into the pond behind our summer cabin at 2 a.m.

Share traditions and pass them on down. We have fairies come to our house after Thanksgiving to stay until Christmas. They do crazy things and have lots of fun with the children, but they only come out at night when everyone is asleep. The kids communicate with them through notes and letters. It's a few weeks of joy for the entire family.

Playing Together ～

Family activities are valuable tools to teach children, as we've discussed. Family play can infuse everyone with love that will ripple through generations to come. Have a weekly family play night or game night. The following ideas are only a springboard to help you create your own family council ideas. Brainstorm together and develop your own fun.

Sports

Recreational sporting events are as numerous and varied as the sands of the sea. Take your family council outside and have some fun. Expose your children to the activities you are interested in, but also listen to what they would like to do. Correlate their abilities with sports they like.

Many children today participate in organized sports, like soccer and baseball. Parents and children alike love supporting and cheering at the games.

Engaging in family sporting activities is a lot of fun, and it's healthy as well. We had great times riding bikes together, canoeing on a local river, renting four-wheelers, and swimming in a nearby lake. Trips to the beach and ocean were also enjoyable. We planned these outings during our family councils, and everyone had a say.

If your children are involved in organized sports, such as soccer or baseball, family council is a good time to talk about your family values:

* How to be a gracious winner
* How to handle losing
* How to dispute a call you don't agree with
* How to get along with coaches and teammates

Enjoy sports as a family. Set goals in your family council meetings, and stay healthy through exercise.

> "Young people need models,
> not critics."
>
> —*John Wooden*

> "Don't let the fear of striking
> out hold you back."
>
> —*Babe Ruth*

Health-Conscious Activities

Getting in shape is a good goal for everyone in the family. This is a wonderful way to vary family council. Kids love to run and play. It's great for adults to join them. Enjoy jump rope, hopscotch, hide-and-seek, tag, flag football, fox and geese, and musical chairs. Swim, hike, jog, ride bikes, and skateboard. (See the previous section on sports.) You get the idea. The sky's the limit.

"Test Your Brain" Games

Sometimes an activity after family council can be as significant as the council itself.

Word searches are lots of fun. Create your own using family names or places. Do the same with crossword puzzles. There are online programs that will make them for you, or you can sit down together and write them yourselves.

We loved to play a memory game. Fill a cookie sheet with familiar items from around the house. If you wish, use holiday items for Christmas or Valentine's Day. Show it to everyone for thirty seconds. Hide the tray and take one item away. The first person to guess the missing item gets to take the next item away.

Use graph paper to make your own Battleship game—but use items the kids are interested in rather than battleships. How about finding hidden planets or galaxies? Use animals the children like or cartoon characters of their choice.

When our kids were little, they loved to keep collections. We hunted for seashells and sand dollars, gathered coins from around the world, and saved postcards and stamps.

Find brainteaser apps for your phone, tablet, or computer. Fun, creative apps are available and can test everyone's mental acuity.

ACTIVITIES ON-THE-GO

Have some simple games ready for the conclusion of family council—or even a lengthy visit to the doctor's office or other waiting times. To play tic-tac-toe, you only need a paper and pencil—or a phone. See how many words you can make from the word *dictionary* or the like. Draw letters on a child's back and have them guess the word the letters make. Dominos have been a favorite in our family over the generations. Play electronically or buy a set. Match them or build a sculpture.

Many of these types of games can be found on the internet to download onto your electronic devices. It's creative to mix and match old-fashioned paper games with electronic ones. One of our favorites is to hunt for Bible verses—some of the family using hard scripture copies while others use electronic ones—and see who can find them first. Sometimes it's a toss-up. Kids will learn from and enjoy both.

I Spy is also fun. It's just like twenty questions, except the group has to guess what someone is looking at. You can play these any time and any place with no equipment necessary.

Pioneer Games

Have an ancestor month for family council. Play pioneer games. My grandmother loved to play hide-the-thimble when she was a child. She made a pick-up sticks game out of lengths of straw. She and her friends created treasure hunts outside, and they pressed or dried flowers for winter decorations. They made wreaths out of pine cones and berries. She loved to create fun stick animals and people out of twigs, pine needles, berries, and leaves. Our kids and grandkids love all these activities.

☙ Growing Together ❧

Family councils don't always need to be solution-focused meetings. Use informal family councils to give your children happy childhood memories and pass on your family values while helping them learn about the world they live in.

Childhood is a time of skill building. There are a lot of great activities that can become teaching moments. Create memories with your children as they grow up. Enjoy the now because, in a flash, little ones become adults and are gone.

Positive Self-Talk

Children learn early to be hard on themselves and others. It's important to contradict negative self-talk and name-calling. Family council is a great place to discuss setting positive-talk goals and find ways to change self-destructive behavior.

Develop a list of affirmations that fit your family. Collect complimentary labels and statements you can use in the following activities.

Here are some games for learning positive self-talk:

* Get rid of garbage words. Fill a "positive" jar with pompoms. Label another jar "garbage." Every time someone says something

negative, or a bad word, they have to take a pompom from the positive jar and put it in the garbage jar. Your goal is to keep all the pompoms in the positive jar. Begin again each week until your family can keep the garbage jar empty. Then have a pizza party, visit a museum, or play at the park.

* Increase your vocabulary. If anyone says a bad word or anything negative about another person, they must find a positive word in the dictionary and bring it to family council for everyone to learn.
* Print a group of positive words on word strips. Cut the word strips into sections and have the family put them back together again. Memorize the meaning of each word.
* Gather a group of positive words and print them on a page, but group the words wrong—put the spaces in the wrong places, like this: Lo veyourneigh b orasyours e lf. Have the family try to guess the right words.
* Scramble the letters of the positive words you want your children to learn.
* Make your own game to fit your family's needs.

> ## "Our happiness depends on the habit of mind we cultivate."
>
> —NORMAN VINCENT PEALE

A VARIETY OF EXPERIENCES

Expose your family to a variety of experiences. For Christmas we like to give gifts to the grandchildren that will last all year long—like season passes to the zoo, science museum, art gallery, or history museum. Have a family council activity at the zoo or museum. What fun for the whole family! Discuss your goals at family council and check the places of interest in your area. Plan a family meeting once a month or once a quarter at a museum or the zoo. It will broaden everyone's view of the world.

If you have a budding playwright, put on a skit. Hold a summer concert for your musicians. Follow it up with an art show. Invite the neighbors and serve refreshments.

Create summer reading contests. Play charades or create special book reports to share with the family. Have the children enjoy some of the classics in children's literature. Then they can give the adults a test on the same books to see how much they remember from their reading of years ago. *Lassie Come Home* is a great one to start with. Many of these books can be downloaded for free.

Plan a vacation to include places everyone in the family will enjoy. Brainstorm anything of interest, including family history trips to visit places your ancestors came from. One of our greatest family reunions was planned around a visit to the Fox Islands off the coast of Maine where some of my husband's ancestors came from. The spirit of the place resonated through our souls. We had found our roots.

> ## "A family is a place where minds come in contact with one another."
>
> —*BUDDHA*

DATE NIGHTS AND VACATIONS

Mom and Dad need to get away and spend time together. Have special family date nights. It's also fun to mix it up a little so Mom and Dad can take each of the children individually for an outing. Let the kids choose the place they want to go. If they love astronomy, enjoy the planetarium together. If they like the ocean, visit the aquarium.

Plan your vacations around the interests of your family. Include activities everyone will enjoy. Study the area before you go so everyone has a working knowledge of what they're going to see. Help the children develop a vacation budget so they'll have spending money on the trip. The planning can be enjoyable and will teach the children as much or more than they'll learn on the trip itself.

There are many other ideas for family fun. Hopefully this sampling will spark your own creative imagination. Find what works for you and create great family memories.

SELF-ESTEEM BUILDERS

Highlight a family member at family council each month. It can be a member of your immediate family or someone living far away. Play "Guess Who" about a family member.

Have a secret pal activity for the month of December or use it for an Easter activity. You can have a special night just for compliments—spoken, crafted, sung, acted out, or any other method you can think of.

A "Caught you being good" bowl is a great way to earn points for a family activity.

SECRET PAL ACTIVITIES

This is a fun way to help kids serve others. Secret pals can be a great part of your Christmas festivities. Structure it any way you want and at any time of the year. A secret valentine or a secret Easter bunny would also be great.

Decide ahead of time what you want the secret person to do:

* Give small, homemade gifts
* Give gifts that cost less than a dollar
* Give secret service

* Leave love notes
* Leave positive messages
* Prepare his or her pal's favorite food
* Help in some small, secret way

Hold a family council activity at the end of the holiday or service time so that the secret pal is revealed (if they haven't already been caught). Everyone will have fun, and everyone will have given thoughtful service.

This is only a small list of ideas. Use your own imagination. You'll be able to come up with creative ideas tailored to your family's likes and talents.

Remember that the activities and ideas aren't the most important. Being together is what matters. Memories don't come from thinking up creative ideas; they come from doing things as a family. A friend once asked his children what some of their favorite childhood memories were. He thought they would say Disneyland vacations or the like. But they remembered things like going to the canyon early on a Saturday morning to build a fire, make scones, and watch the sunrise.

TOKEN ECONOMY

Use your family council meetings to set family behavior goals. A token economy is a wonderful way to shape actions. It can be used as a means of altering the way children conduct themselves with positive reinforcement. Family councils give a time for setting goals, a time for accountability, and a time for evaluation.

1. Decide the target behavior you want to change.
2. Have the family set up the reward (a trip to the zoo, a pizza party, etc.).
3. Decide who will keep track of the behavior changes.
   a. Mom or Dad can track the behaviors.
   b. Each child can track his own.

4. Choose the system you want to use. The system can be as creative and varied as you wish:

a. Put marbles, beans, poker chips, gold coins, pennies, tickets, etc. in a jar.

b. Create a chart and put stickers, thumb tacks, stars, etc. on the chart.

c. Use play money (such as Monopoly money) or make your own.

d. Make "Good Job" coupons.

e. Use phone and internet apps if you wish. They are fun, and kids can track their progress.

Kids love using this type of a reward system. Many of them are familiar with it because it's so common in school. If you find this works for your family, change it fairly often. Our kids loved variety in their work charts and their token economy.

> # "Nothing you do for children is ever wasted."
>
> —GARRISON KEILLOR

Chapter 6:

Fostering Maturity

ᕦ Consideration ᕤ

Children learn how to build relationships in the context of the family. If we are considerate of each other, they will be also. Getting along with family members is of prime importance, and family councils are a place to teach consideration and follow through on reaffirming that message.

I once saw a couple in counseling where the husband stated flatly that he would not argue with his wife, and he stayed true to that principle. She had come from a family where there was constant discord, and she had to learn a new way of living. It was difficult for her, but she did it. I have kept in touch with that family over the years, and they are kind and loving to each other. The children have compassion and consideration for those around them.

Show concern for each other.

When someone is sad or in crisis, take a few minutes to listen to their feelings.

Don't discount children's feelings.

I learned this lesson the hard way. When our girls were in their teens, they would sit down to visit with me, saying, "I'm not pretty, like Jane or Sally."

I would always respond, "Oh, yes you are. You are. You are beautiful."

I thought I was doing a good thing, but I learned that I was discounting their feelings. The girls wouldn't talk to me about their feelings because I wasn't really hearing them—until one of them told me I wasn't really listening.

The next week at family council, we talked about observing others' feelings. After that, I changed my ways for the better. (Aren't you glad for your children? They teach you so many important life lessons as they grow up.)

Whether at family council or not, learn to listen to and acknowledge kids' feelings before sharing your own.

TREAT EACH MEMBER OF THE FAMILY LOVINGLY.

I think it can be easy to love infants. As children grow and have temper tantrums and come home muddy and forget to clean up after themselves, it's a little more challenging to hold and hug them. A sweaty, smelly ten-year-old who is devastated because his team just lost the championship game needs some support. So hug him!

I believe the minimum daily requirement is four hugs per day for every person in your family. That's a lot of great hugging!

As our children were growing up, I hope I treated everyone with love and kindness (most of the time). I wasn't perfect, but I tried.

Family council was a good place for me to check myself. Was I favoring one child over another? I hope not, but listen to yourself and get feedback from other members of your family.

TEACH CHILDREN ABOUT SERVICE.

Family councils are a great place to create and plan service projects. I do not believe one can be truly happy without giving service to the world in some way or another. Caring for others is the basis for loving relationships. We must give and accept love in order to be happy.

One of the greatest blessings we received in our family was the opportunity to care for my grandmother and later my grandfather in our home until their deaths.

There are so many ways to serve others:

* In your family
* In your neighborhood
* In your community
* In your church
* In your school

The list could go on and on. Make a difference in your world. Give to those around you and endow your children with an even greater gift—happiness.

☙ STRUCTURE ❧

Families will order their lives in very different ways. If we were to line up fifty families and ask them how they went about organizing their days, we would get fifty varied answers. And that would be fine. Every family has its own personality and must function in a way that suits it best. Family councils are a great place to design that structure.

Even in our immediate family, our grown children order their families differently. Some of our children are meticulously focused on the particulars of the event in process—planning it out to the last detail. And others let things flow freely, according to the moment.

Family councils help us maintain a sense of consistency in life.

SECURITY COMES FROM ROUTINE.

Small children find a sense of safety in knowing there is a steady routine in their lives. From infancy, they enjoy a consistent nap time. This changes, of course, as the child grows, but it's nice for them to know predictability.

Family councils are a place to set the family standards and decide on a schedule that will work for everyone. Whether it's meal times, sleep routines, chore charts, or school and work calendars—family meetings are a great place to plan.

We moved fairly often when the children were small. So when my husband received his new assignment, we spent a couple of meetings talking about the new place we would live and the fun things there would be to do in the new area of the country. We talked about when and how we would relocate, and the kids helped decide the travel plans.

There are times for all families when crisis comes. These meetings are a good time to let everyone know what's going to happen or let them help decide the events that should follow. As our family has grown and expanded to the next generation, we keep in touch through family emails and texts. When someone is in the hospital or critically ill, nightly emails give everyone an update.

CHILDREN HAVE A SAY IN FAMILY HAPPENINGS.

When a family does move, family council is a great time for everyone to look online at schools' test scores, athletic programs, extra-curricular activities, and the like to find a good location to live.

A family I worked with had a son receive an honor from the governor of the state. The entire family scheduled a vacation around the award ceremonies and had a great time together.

Many families love to take trips to Disneyland or Disney World. Give the kids a say in the incidentals. Brainstorm ways they can earn spending money. Let them help choose the hotel and other amenities. Great side trips abound in both California and Florida. Discuss the different options available to your family and let the entire group plan the itinerary.

TEACH GIVE-AND-TAKE.

In all this planning, everyone in the family will learn about give-and-take. Cooperation is a wonderful skill for children to learn, and it will stand them in good places as they launch themselves into the work force in years to come.

Negotiation skills are important for us all—an important gift to give your entire family that can be facilitated by your family meetings.

✂ RESPECT ✂

As we listen to each other and work together, we are sending an underlying message of respect for those around us. Through council meetings, discussions, and negotiations, we say to our family members, "I love you and respect you."

This happens as we do these things:

Talk to each other.

Consider each other's feedback as important.

There are so many valuable lessons that come from this process for the child:

* I am important.
* What I say is of value.
* I have good ideas.
* You respect me.

But the most significant effect the family council process has on children is this: they grow in the definition of who they are in the context of your family values.

Councils help children gain a strong sense of self and family.

✎ BONDING ✎

Writing this book has been a great experience for me. I've loved review-ing experiences from my own family, friend's families, and families of my clients. I'm sure as you've read through these pages, you've thought of your own childhood and family experiences.

There are so many wonderful messages we give to ourselves and our children through this family council process, but the greatest is the gift of loving each other.

* You have treasured me enough to guide my life.
* You have cared for me enough to structure my environment.
* You are devoted enough to listen to me.
* You appreciate me enough to consider my ideas.
* You respect me enough to help me learn from my mistakes.
* You cherish me enough to teach me your values.
* You love me.

Love is at the core of every good thing in the world. Make it your core.

My role as a mother has changed since we held our first family council meeting so many years ago. I no longer have to scurry around to care for a large group of people. I don't have to organize them anymore. I can just love them, respect the adults they have become, and love their children.

Enjoy the time you have with little ones in your home. Appreciate each moment. Family brings joy into our lives that just gets better and better.

I have learned over the years that family talk in family councils is a wonderful way to foster relationships. They can create a positive setting for the family to understand and resolve problems. The productive ener-gy emanating from these meetings will help you and your children add light and goodness to your environment wherever you go.

Quote Sources

Beattie, Melody. *Beyond Codependency: And Getting Better All the Time*. Minnesota: Hazelden Foundation, 1989. Print

Beliefnet. Beliefnet, Inc. Last modified 2013. http://beliefnet.com

Brainy Quote. BookRags Media Network. Last modified 2013. http://www.brainyquote.com

Campbell, Joseph. *Reflections on the Art of Living*. New York: HarperCollins, 1991. Print.

Emerson, Ralph Waldo. "The Sovereignty of Ethics." *North American Review* 10.12 (1878): 175–206. Web.

Feiler, Bruce. "The Stories That Bind Us." March 15, 2013. http://www.nytimes.com/2013/03/17/fashion/the-family-stories-that-bind-us-this-life.html?_r=0

Frank, Anne. *The Diary of Anne Frank*. Geneva: Doubleday, 1967. Print.

Good Reads. Goodreads, Inc. Last modified 2013. http://www.goodreads.com

Merton, Thomas. *No Man Is an Island*. Boston: Shambhala Publications, 1955. Print.

Miéville, China. *The Scar*. New York: The Random House Publishing Group, 2002. Print.

Oliver, Mary. "It Was Early." *Evidence*. Boston: Beacon Press, 2009. Print.

Oliver, Mary. "The Uses of Sorrow." *Thirst: Poems*. Boston: Beacon Press, 2006. Print.

Quotations Book. Last Modified 2013. http://quotationsbook.com

Quotations Page, The. QuotationsPage.com and Michael Moncur. Last modified 2013. http://quotationspage.com

Schweitzer, Albert. "The Meaning of Ideals in Life." Silcoates School. Wakefield, England. 3 December 1935.

Search Quotes. Last modified 2013. http://searchquotes.com/

Think Exist. Last modified 2013. http://thinkexist.com

Warren, Elizabeth. *All Your Worth*. New York: Free Press, 2005. Print.

Wikiquote. Last modified 2013. http://en.wikiquote.org

About the Author

Christy Monson received a B.S. degree at Utah State University and an M.S. at University of Nevada at Las Vegas. She established a successful counseling practice in Las Vegas, Nevada, as a Licensed Marriage and Family Therapist, spending a great portion of her time working with young people and their families. She and her husband, Robert have raised six children and have fourteen grandchildren.

She has written a children's book series, *Texting Through Time*, and has a picture book, *Love, Hugs, and Hope When Scary Things Happen*, released September 1 of 2013. Her self help book, *Becoming Free, A Woman's Guide to Internal Strength* was also released September 1, 2013,

Her articles have been published on the web in Familius, Gospel Ideals, LDS Witness, Modern Molly Mormon, and American Night Writer's Association. Her blog address is:

http://christymonson.blogspot.com/

Her websites are:

http://www.christymonson.com/index.html and

http://textingthroughtime.com/.

Like her author page:

http://www.facebook.com/christymonsonauthor?v=wall

About Familius

Welcome to a place where mothers are celebrated, not compared. Where heart is at the center of our families, and family at the center of our homes. Where boo boos are still kissed, cake beaters are still licked, and mistakes are still okay. Welcome to a place where books—and family—are beautiful. Familius: a book publisher dedicated to helping families be happy.

Familius was founded in 2012 with the intent to align the founders' love of publishing and family with the digital publishing renaissance which occurred simultaneously with the Great Recession. The founders believe that the traditional family is the basic unit of society, and that a society is only as strong as the families that create it. Familius's mission is to help families be happy. We invite you to participate with us in strengthening your family by being part of the Familius family.

Join Our Family!

By subscribing to the Familius monthly newsletter, you'll learn ideas to help your family, receive special discounts and free giveaways on Familius products, a free monthly ebook, and be the first to learn about our Let's Talk Family conferences. Subscribe by going to familius.com And, if you want more frequent ideas to help you and your family be inspired, subscribe to the Familius blog.

Visit Our Website: www.familius.com

Our website is a different kind of place—all focused around helping your family be happy. Read articles, read books, watch videos, contact our family experts, download books and apps and audio books, and more.

Become an Expert

Familus authors and other established writers interested in helping families be happy are invited to join our online family and contribute online content. If you have something important to say on the family, join our expert community help families be happy.

Get Bulk Discounts

If you feel a few friends and family might benefit from what you've read, let us know and we're happy to provide you with quantity discounts. Simply email us at specialorders@familius.com.

Website: www.familius.com

Facebook: www.facebook.com/paterfamilius

Twitter: @familiustalk, @paterfamilius1

Pinterest: www.pinterest.com/familius

CPSIA information can be obtained at www.ICGtesting.com
Printed in the USA
BVOW01s1904100414

350177BV00004B/7/P